# Basic ESL
## *Workbook*

The companion book to Basic ESL *Online*:
www.basicesl.com

### LEVEL 3

C. Sesma, M. A.
ESL and Spanish Teacher

Bilingual Dictionaries, Inc.

**Basic ESL® Workbook: Level 3**
**English as a Second Language**

**Publisher:**
**Bilingual Dictionaries, Inc.**
P.O. Box 1154
Murrieta, CA 92564
Website: www.bilingualdictionaries.com
Email: support@bilingualdictionaries.com

**Content** by C. Sesma, M.A.
English and Spanish Teacher

**Design** by John Garcia

ISBN13: 978-0-933146-38-9
ISBN: 0-933146-38-8

The **Basic ESL® Workbooks** are the companion books to **Basic ESL® Online.**
Basic ESL Online provides:
> Online English Learning
> Audio Pronunciation of English
> Native Language Support

For **information** and **registration** to Basic ESL® Online please visit the the Basic ESL® website:
**Website: www.BasicESL.com**
**Email: info@basicesl.com**

# *Prologue*

The **Basic ESL Workbook** is the companion book to **Basic ESL Online (www.basicesl.com)**. Except for the English pronunciations and native language translations that are provided online, this book follows the online course content with some adjustments required by the book format. Since written grammatical exercises cannot be provided online, this book has added an extra section at the end of each lesson. The written exercises section provides the ability to test the student's progress and knowledge of the English language structure. In order for the student to get the best of Basic ESL, it is very important to be familiar with the goals and learning methods of the online lessons found at www.basicesl.com.

The **main goal** of Basic ESL Online is to develop the oral skills of communication rather than trying to memorize grammatical rules. The first oral skill of communication is **to be able to understand the spoken English**. This is accomplished by continuous listening to the oral exercises, stories, dialogs and conversations. The second and most important oral skill of communication is **to be able to ask and answer questions.**

To accomplish these goals, Basic ESL offers simple and effective learning methods that will help the student succeed in learning English as a Second Language:

**1. The gradual, step by step approach of learning the English language**. Each lesson is built on the knowledge of the previous lessons, in addition to the new content for that lesson.

**2. The Lesson Sections (A-H):** the vocabulary study, the sentence structure, the listening exercises, the conversation exercises and the presentation of common phrases used by native English speakers.

**3. The English Pronunciation**. At Basic ESL Online, the students are in control of the English pronunciation by allowing them to listen and repeat all the words and sentences as many times as needed.

**4. The Translations**. The translation of the English vocabulary and sentence structures into the native language of the student will speed up the process of learning English. The translations are also a great tool for self-study at home or at the local library.

**5. The Explanation of Grammatical Concepts.** Students who want to learn the mechanics of the language will find grammar concepts explained in their native language. By clicking on the **information button** ℹ️ at Basic ESL Online, students can view the translated grammar concepts that go along with the lesson.

The Basic ESL Workbook works together with Basic ESL Online (www.basicesl.com) to give English language learners a simple and effective way to learn English as a second language. Basic ESL Online provides the audio English pronunciation for the different lesson sections as well as the written native language translations. We strongly recommend all Basic ESL students to register for Basic ESL Online at www.basicesl.com.

# Recommendation to the Student

In order to obtain the best results from the use of this Basic ESL Workbook, we recommend the student becomes a member of **Basic ESL Online** at:

## www.basicesl.com

Here the student will find the audio English pronunciations, the native language translation support of the vocabulary and the sentence structures, plus the grammar explanations in the language of the student.

# Contents

# Chapter 1
# Countryside

# What to do in each section of every lesson...

## A - Vocabulary Study

Section A includes the vocabulary that will be used throughout the lesson. Learning new vocabulary is basic to learning a new language.

**Read** the vocabulary several times.
If you are on Basic ESL Online:
**Listen** to the **English audio pronunciation**.
**View** the **native language translations** of the vocabulary.

Listen and read the vocabulary until you can understand the vocabulary without looking at the words.

## B - Sentence Structure

Section B teaches students basic English sentences using the vocabulary in section A.

**Read** and **study** the sentences.
If you are on Basic ESL Online:
**Listen** to the **English audio pronunciation**.
**View** the **native language translations** of the sentences.
**View** the **grammar concepts** by clicking on the **information button** .

Repeat the sentences as many times as needed.
Continue to the next section once you can **understand** the sentences without looking at them.

## C - Listening Exercises

**Read** the story or dialog several times.
If you are on Basic ESL Online, **listen** to the story or dialog while reading it several times.

Once you are familiar with the story or dialog, try to see if you can **understand** it by only listening without reading.

## D - Conversation Exercises

**Read** the conversation dialogs several times.
If you are on Basic ESL Online, **listen** to the dialogs until you can understand them without looking at them.

Finally, try to **speak** the conversation dialogs by only looking at the pictures and key words.

## E - Common Phrases

Many of the **common phrases** that are presented in this section are frequently used by the native English speakers in their everyday life.

**Read** the common phrases several times.
If you are on Basic ESL Online, **listen** to the common phrases while reading. **Listen** as many times as needed until you can understand the common phrases without looking at the sentences.

## H - Written Exercises

The written exercises provide an opportunity to test what you learned in the lesson. You can never be sure of knowing something unless you can put it in writing.

You can check your answers by going to the **Answer Key Section** in the back of the workbook.

For information regarding **Basic ESL Online,** please visit **www.basicesl.com**.
Audio Pronunciaton of English & Native Language Translations.

# Lesson #1

## Trees, Plants & Flowers

## Index

### Audio & Translations

 **English Audio available online for sections A-E.**

 **Translations in various Languages available online for Sections A, B, and E.**

**www.BasicESL.com**

**1.** rose

**2.** carnation

**3.** lily

**4.** daisy

**5.** tulip

**6.** magnolia

**7.** violet

**8.** lilac

**9.** sunflower

**10.** tree

**11.** branch

**12.** bamboo

**13.** oak tree

**14.** palm tree

**15.** juniper

**16.** olive tree

**17.** pine tree

**18.** cactus

## Vocabulary Study: Other Vocabulary

| 1. | n | air | 11. | adj | uncommon |
|----|-----|----------|-----|-----|-----------|
| 2. | n | country | 12. | v | cover |
| 3. | n | elk | 13. | v | erupt |
| 4. | n | geyser | 14. | v | fill |
| 5. | n | herd | 15. | v | hike |
| 6. | n | spring | 16. | v | hunt |
| 7. | n | waterfall | 17. | v | reach |
| 8. | adj | filled | 18. | v | shoot |
| 9. | adj | grizzly | 19. | v | sightsee |
| 10. | adj | native | 20. | adv | a year ago |

For the audio pronunciations and written translations of **Sections A and B,** please go to:

**www.basicesl.com**

## Vocabulary Study: Other Vocabulary

| 1. | n | example | 11. | v | deal |
|----|-----|-----------|-----|-----|------------|
| 2. | n | peace | 12. | v | demand |
| 3. | n | slope | 13. | v | develop |
| 4. | n | summit | 14. | v | enable |
| 5. | adj | attractive | 15. | v | matter |
| 6. | adj | delicate | 16. | v | prevent |
| 7. | adj | fertile | 17. | v | require |
| 8. | adj | flat | 18. | v | strengthen |
| 9. | adj | hollow | 19. | v | warn |
| 10. | adj | slippery | 20. | v | weaken |

## B1.  Superlative Form (S):  Short Adjectives

The pine tree is **tall**.
S   It is **the tallest** tree **in** the patio.

The Nile river is **long**.
S   It is **the longest** river **in** Africa.

Roses are **pretty** flowers.
S   They're **the prettiest of** all.

Ray is a **strong** boy.
S   He's **the strongest in** class.

## B2.  Superlative Form: Long Adjectives

Jane is a **polite** girl.
S   She's **the most polite of** all.

Mr. Hank is a **powerful** man.
S   He's **the most powerful in** the city.

This movie is **horrible**.
S   It's **the most horrible in** town.

Tulips are **popular** flowers.
S   They're **the most popular of** all.

## B3.  Comparisons: Superiority (s) and Superlative (S)

You are **short**.
s   You are **shorter than** Sharon.
S   You are **the shortest in** the class.

Sara is **polite**.
s   She is **more polite** than Ray.
S   She is **the most polite of** all.

The book is **heavy**.
s   The box is **heavier than** the book.
S   The table is **the heaviest of** the three.

### B1 - B2 - B3

*The superlative form of the adjective is used to indicate the highest degree of quality among three or more people, things or places. The superlative comparison is formed two ways depending on the number of syllables of the adjective.*

*Short adjectives, with one or two syllables, form the superlative form by adding "-est" to the adjective.*

*Long adjectives with three or more syllables, and two syllable adjectives not ending in "-y," form the superlative degree with the word "most" in front of the adjective.*

*In the last part of the comparison, the preposition "in" or "at" is used when followed by a place. We use "of" when the adjective is followed by words expressing a number.*

## B4. Comparisons: Irregular Forms

|   | |
|---|---|
|   | Phoenix is **far** from Las Vegas. |
| S | Dallas is **farther** than Phoenix. |
| s | Miami is **the farthest of** the three. |
|   | Chicken is a **good** dish. |
| S | It is **better** than pork. |
| s | It is **the best dish in** the restaurant. |
|   | Andy is a **bad** student. |
| S | He is **worse than** Tony. |
| s | He is **the worst student in** class. |

**B4 - B5**

*The adjectives "**far, good, bad, many**" and "**little**" have irregular superlative forms.*

## B5. Comparisons: Irregular Forms

Tony has **a lot of** money.
  Casey has **more** money than Tony.
  Fred has **the most** money of all.

Sara has **little** money.
  You have **less money** than Sara.
  I have **the least** money of all.

Susan has **many** toys
  Ann has **more** toys than Susan.
  Lucy has **the most** toys of all.

## B6. "do", "does" and "did" for emphasis (E)

|   | |
|---|---|
|   | **Do** you **clean** your clothes? |
|   | Yes, I **clean** my clothes. |
| E | Yes, I **do clean** my clothes. |
|   | **Does** Fred **work** here? |
|   | Yes, he **works** here. |
| E | Yes, he **does work** here. |
|   | **Did** the girl **finish** Level 2? |
|   | Yes, she **finished** Level 2. |
| E | Yes, she **did finish** Level 2. |

**B6**

*The auxiliary verbs "**do, does**" and "**did**" are not normally used in affirmative statements. However they are used sometimes for **emphasis**. In this case, they are followed by the base form of the main verb.*

## C1. Read and Listen to the story.

Yellowstone National Park is one the most famous parks in the United States. It was the first national park in the world. The Native Americans were hunting and fishing there over 11,000 years ago. Yellowstone covers about 3,500 square miles. It is filled with lakes, rivers and mountains. Over 90% of the park is located in the state of Wyoming. There are over 290 waterfalls inside the park.

It contains many geysers. A geyser is a spring of hot water shooting into the air. One of them reaches 300 feet high. The most famous of them is the Old Faithful. Yellowstone is home to grizzly bears, wolves, and herds of bison and elk. It is not uncommon to see the bears in the middle of the road when driving through the park. Over two million people visit the park every year and enjoy fishing, hiking and sightseeing.

## C2. Read and Listen to the story.

***What is the name of one of the most famous parks in the United States?***
Its name is Yellowstone National Park.

***Is this park the biggest park in the country?***
No, it is not. There are bigger parks in the country.

***In what part of the country is it located?***
Ninety percent of the park is located in the state of Wyoming.

***What does the park contain in its 3,500 square miles?***
It contains many lakes, rivers, waterfalls and geysers.

***How many waterfalls are there in the park?***
There are 290 waterfalls in the park.

**D1.** tall (juniper) / forest

**Is the pine tree tall?**
 Yes, it is very tall.

**Is it taller than the juniper?**
 Yes, it is taller.

**How tall do you think it is?**
 It is the tallest tree in the forest.

**D2.** colorful (daisy) / all

**Is the rose colorful?**
 Yes, it is very colorful.

**Is it more colorful than the daisy?**
 Yes, it is more colorful.

**How colorful do you think it is?**
 It is the most colorful flower of all.

**D3.** expensive (violet) / store

**Is the tulip expensive?**
 Yes, it is expensive.

**Is it more expensive than the violet?**
 Yes, it is more expensive.

**How expensive do you think it is?**
 It is the most expensive flower at the store.

**D4.** strong (olive tree) / all

**Is the oak tree strong?**
 Yes, it is strong.

**Is it stronger than the olive tree?**
 Yes, it is stronger.

**How strong do you think it is?**
 It is the strongest tree of all.

## Verb "to go"

1. **Go on.**
2. I want to **go out** for a moment.
3. Don't **go down** to the basement.
4. We like to **go up** the hill.
5. Let's **go over** the results.
6. Suddenly the bomb **goes off**.
7. She **goes along** with my plan.
8. **Go back** home and rest.
9. **Go ahead** with your plans.
10. The business can **go under**.

**Phrasal verbs** or **prepositional verbs** are verbs followed by a preposition or an adverb. When the verb is followed by a preposition or adverb, the verb acquires a different meaning from the original meaning. When the object of the phrasal verb is a direct object pronoun, the pronoun is placed between the verb and the preposition.

For the English audio pronunciations and written native language translations of **section E**, please go to:

# www.basicesl.com

I want **to go out** for a moment.

Let's **go over** the results.

End of the **oral exercises** for lesson 1.
**You can find additional exercises in sections D, F & G at Basic ESL Online.**

Please continue with the **written exercises** for this lesson in **section H**.

Lesson

1

**H1.** Write the comparative and superlative form of these adjectives.

| | | | |
|---|---|---|---|
| 1. | strong | *stronger than* | *the strongest of (in)* |
| 2. | easy | | |
| 3. | nice | | |
| 4. | big | | |
| 5. | bad | | |
| 6. | beautiful | | |
| 7. | unhappy | | |
| 8. | large | | |
| 9. | small | | |
| 10. | pretty | | |
| 11. | good | | |
| 12. | heavy | | |
| 13. | far | | |
| 14. | dangerous | | |
| 15. | many | | |
| 16. | little | | |
| 17. | colorful | | |
| 18. | fertile | | |

## H2. Make comparisons.

1. pine tree / tall tree / all
   *The pine tree is the tallest tree of all.*

2. oak wood / expensive wood / store
   _____

3. bamboo / ugly tree / all
   _____

4. cactus / dangerous plant / garden
   _____

5. roses / beautiful flowers / market
   _____

6. Cindy / smart girl / three sisters
   _____

## H3. Complete the sentences with: *in, at* or *of.*

1. Tony is the youngest … the family.                               *in*

2. Phillip is the best student … his class.                         _____

3. Frank is the most polite student … all.                          _____

4. The rose is the most beautiful flower … the garden.              _____

5. The size 45 is the biggest size … the store.                     _____

6. The juniper is the tallest tree … all.                           _____

7. My aunt is nice. She is the nicest … all my relatives.           _____

8. This box is the heaviest box … the room.                         _____

9. This mountain is the highest … Germany.                          _____

10. The Nile is the longest … all the rivers.                       _____

11. This classroom is the nicest … the school.                      _____

## H4. Complete the sentences.

1. Margaret is … sweet as her sister.                                    *as*
2. Ruby is 59 years old. Jane is 60 years old. Ruby is … than Jane.    _____
3. Flowers are … expensive than ivy.                                  _____
4. That plant is … beautiful of all.                                 _____
5. The snake is … dangerous animal in the garden.                     _____
6. It is … dangerous than the spider.                                _____
7. The fern is as attractive … any bush.                             _____
8. Who is the … handsome in the family?                              _____
9. My brother is  richer … my sister.                                _____

## H5. Complete the sentences.

1. **Ray is a**     *bad*                        **boy.**
   He is        _____    than Albert.
   He is        _____    in the class.

2. **The school is**   *far*                     **from here.**
   The hospital is  _____   than the school.
   The church is   _____    of the three.

3. **Jane is a**    *good*                        **girl.**
   She is       _____     than Albert.
   She is       _____     in the class.

4. **Debbie has**   *a lot of*                    **money.**
   Becky has    _____     money than Debbie.
   Nancy has    _____     money of the three.

5. **I spend**      *little*                       **money.**
   Ricky spends  _____    money than I.
   My sons spend  _____   money at home.

## H6. Follow the example.

1.  big / zoo

    **dog**
    **lion**
    **giraffe**

    *The dog is **big**.*
    *The lion is **bigger** than the dog.*
    *The giraffe is the **biggest** animal in the zoo.*

2.  tall / forest

    **olive tree**
    **oak tree**
    **pine tree**

    _____
    _____
    _____
    _____

3.  aggressive / three

    **boar**
    **bear**
    **tiger**

    _____
    _____
    _____
    _____

4.  pretty / all

    **lily**
    **daisy**
    **tulip**

    _____
    _____
    _____
    _____

5.  good / restaurant

    **cheese**
    **pie**
    **apple**

    _____
    _____
    _____
    _____

# Lesson #2

## The Garden

## Index

## Audio & Translations

 English Audio available online for sections A-E.

 Translations in various Languages available online for Sections A, B, and E.

## www.BasicESL.com

**1.** wheel barrow

**2.** pick

**3.** lawn mower

**4.** rake

**5.** spade

**6.** hoe

**7.** fork

**8.** shovel

**9.** pot

**10.** shears

**11.** to dig *(a hole)*

**12.** to plant

**13.** to water

**14.** to trim *(plants)*

**15.** to pull *(weeds)*

**16.** to trim *(a bush)*

**17.** to prune *(the branches)*

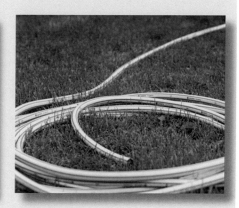

**18.** hose

## Vocabulary Study: Other Vocabulary

| | | | | | | |
|---|---|---|---|---|---|---|
| 1. | n | bag | 11. | v | take care |
| 2. | n | garden | 12. | v | maintain |
| 3. | n | hole | 13. | v | pick up |
| 4. | n | leaf | 14. | v | fill |
| 5. | n | nursery | 15. | v | pull out |
| 6. | n | orchard | 16. | v | put |
| 7. | n | trash | 17. | v | weigh |
| 8. | n | weeds | 18. | adv | afterwards |
| 9. | adj | light | 19. | adv | fairly |
| 10. | adj | neat | 20. | adv | in charge of |

For the audio pronunciations and written translations of **Sections A and B,** please go to:

## www.basicesl.com

## Vocabulary Study: Other Vocabulary

| | | | | | | |
|---|---|---|---|---|---|---|
| 1. | n | pride | 11. | v | commit |
| 2. | adj | alive | 12. | v | concern |
| 3. | adj | crooked | 13. | v | contribute |
| 4. | adj | dead | 14. | v | discuss |
| 5. | adj | helpful | 15. | v | expect |
| 6. | adj | lively | 16. | v | handle |
| 7. | adj | numerous | 17. | v | provide |
| 8. | adj | proud | 18. | v | reveal |
| 9. | adj | substantial | 19. | con | so that |
| 10. | adj | thrifty | 20. | con | whether |

## B1. Regular Verbs: Past Tense

**ℹ️**

Sue always **waters** the flowers.
Yesterday she water**ed** the shrubs.

They always **plant** trees.
Yesterday they plant**ed** a juniper.

Tom always **cleans** the orchard.
Sara clean**ed** the orchard yesterday.

We always **pick up** the leaves.
Paul **picked up** the leaves yesterday.

## B2. Irregular Verbs: Past Tense: Negative Sentences

**ℹ️**

| | |
|---|---|
| **burst** | The pipe **burst** yesterday. <br> It didn't **burst** today. |
| **dig** | We **dug** three holes. <br> We **didn't dig** ten holes. |
| **buy** | Ann **bought** plastic bags. <br> She **didn't buy** paper bags. |
| **break** | She **broke** a pot. <br> She **didn't break** a glass. |

## B3. Irregular Verbs: Past Tense: Negative Sentences

| | |
|---|---|
| **cost** | The lawn mower **cost** a lot. <br> It didn't **cost** $10.00. |
| **burn** | Alex **burnt** the trash. <br> He didn't **burn** the weeds. |
| **build** | They **built** a house. <br> They didn't **build** a cottage. |
| **bring** | I **brought** some trees. <br> I **didn't bring** flowers. |

### B1

*Regular verbs* are those that form the simple **past tense** and **past participle** by adding "**-ed**" to the verb.

*Irregular verbs* are those which do not follow the rule above. The verbs may have different forms in the past tense and in the past participle. Some verbs have the same irregular form for the past tense and for the past participle. Other verbs have different forms.

### B2 - B3

*The irregular verbs* form negative sentences in the **past tense** with "**did not**", followed by the basic form of the main verb.

## B4. Irregular and Regular Verbs: **Questions and Answers**

*Did you **catch** any worms?*
   Yes, I **caught** some worms.

*Did your dad **cut** any bushes?*
   Yes, he **cut** only one bush.

*Did Fred **choose** this rake?*
   Yes, he **chose** this rake.

*Did you **plant** any trees today?*
   Yes, I **planted** some trees today.

**B4**

*Questions in the past tense with irregular verbs start with "**Did**" + **subject** + the **basic form of the verb**, which is the same for all subjects.*

## B5. Regular and Irregular Verbs: **Questions and Answers**

*Did the dog **bite** the children?*
   The dog **bit** the boy.
   It **didn't bite** the girl.

*Did Henry **pull** out the weeds?*
   He **pulled** out some weeds.
   He **didn't pull** out all the weeds.

*Did you **blow** out the candles?*
   I **blew** out only one candle.
   I **did not blow** out all the candles.

## B6. List of irregular Verbs

*Did you **come** early?*
   Yes, I **came** early.

*Did you **foresee** all this?*
   Yes, I **foresaw** all this.

*Did your parents **bet** a lot of money?*
   Yes, they **bet** a lot of money.

*Did the man **bend** the iron bar?*
   Yes, he **bent** the iron bar.

## C1. Read and Listen to the Story.

**Last Saturday** Charles, my oldest son, **was** in charge of maintaining the garden neat and clean. He **started** to work in the garden early. First of all, he **trimmed** the bushes and the trees. Afterwards, he **dug** a few holes in the ground. Then Charles **planted** some trees and flowers. He **purchased** the plants from the nursery.

Afterwards he **pulled** out the weeds. He **use**d a light hoe and a pick. When he **finished** pulling out the weeds, he **picked up** the leaves from the ground. He **put** the trash in plastic bags. The kitchen white bags are fairly big, but the black garden bags are bigger. They are the biggest of all the plastic bags.

**Last Saturday**, Chuck **filled** three plastic bags with trash. Each one **weighed** 35 pounds. After picking up the trash, Chuck **mowed** lawn. Alex, his younger brother, **watered** the plants.

## C2. Read and Listen to the dialog.

*Who is Charles?*
> He is the oldest son in the family.

*What did he do last Saturday?*
> He took care of the garden.

*What did he do first?*
> He trimmed the bushes.

*Did he dig any holes?*
> Yes, he dug a few holes.

*Did he plant any flowers?*
> Yes, he planted some flowers.

*What did he do next?*
> He pulled out the weeds.

*Where did he put the trash?*
> He put the trash in plastic bags.

*What kind of bags did he use?*
> He used big garden bags.

*What color were they?*
> They were black.

*How much did they weigh?*
> They weighed 35 pounds each.

**D1.** Carl / year

**What is Carl doing?**
   He is planting a tree.

**How often does he plant trees?**
   He plants trees every year.

**Did he plant a tree last year?**
   Yes, he planted a tree last year.

**D2.** mother / day

**What is your mother doing?**
   She is watering the flowers.

**How often does she water the flowers?**
   She waters the flowers every day.

**Did she water the flowers yesterday?**
   Yes, she watered the flowers yesterday.

**D3.** brothers / month

**What are the brothers doing?**
   They are trimming the bushes.

**How often do they trim the bushes?**
   They trim the bushes every month.

**Did they trim the bushes last month?**
   Yes, they trimmed the bushes.

**D4.** Sara / semester

**What is Sara doing?**
   She is digging a hole.

**How often does she dig a hole?**
   She digs a hole every semester.

**Did she dig a hole last semester?**
   Yes, she dug a hole last semester.

## Verb "to come"

1. **Come back** any time.
2. Can you **come over** tomorrow.
3. Open the door and **come in**.
4. The marriage **came apart**.
5. She **comes across as** sincere.
6. It **came about** this way.
7. The problem **comes down to** this.
8. My dad **came along** with me.
9. I **came upon** my cousin.
10. Something **came up** today.

**Phrasal verbs** or **prepositional verbs** are verbs followed by a preposition or an adverb. When the verb is followed by a preposition or adverb, the verb acquires a different meaning from the original meaning. When the object of the phrasal verb is a direct object pronoun, the pronoun is placed between the verb and the preposition.

For the English audio pronunciations and written native language translations of **section E,** please go to:

## www.basicesl.com

She **comes across** as sincere.

My dad **came along** with me.

End of the **oral exercises** for lesson 2.
**You can find additional exercises in sections D, F & G at Basic ESL Online.**

Please continue with the **written exercises** for this lesson in **section H.**

Lesson

2

## H1. Write the past tense of these verbs.

| | | | | | |
|---|---|---|---|---|---|
| 1. | cost | _____ | build | _____ |
| 2. | cover | _____ | bet | _____ |
| 3. | dig | _____ | handle | _____ |
| 4. | fill | _____ | put | _____ |
| 5. | catch | _____ | cut | _____ |
| 6. | maintain | _____ | weigh | _____ |
| 7. | pick | _____ | discuss | _____ |
| 8. | place | _____ | blow | _____ |
| 9. | plant | _____ | commit | _____ |
| 10. | choose | _____ | break | _____ |
| 11. | prevent | _____ | reveal | _____ |
| 12. | provide | _____ | expect | _____ |
| 13. | buy | _____ | bend | _____ |
| 14. | pull | _____ | water | _____ |
| 15. | trim | _____ | bring | _____ |
| 16. | do | _____ | strengthen | _____ |

## H2. Make the sentences negative.

1. He **planted** a tree.                *He **did not plant** a tree.*
2. We **broke** two picks.              _____
3. Mary **did** homework.               _____
4. She **played** at school.            _____
5. We **built** that house.             _____
6. The house **cost** a lot.            _____
7. They **dug** three holes.            _____
8. The pot **weighed** 20 lbs.          _____
9. She **broke** the rake.              _____
10. Fred **caught** a fish.             _____
11. Mom **trimmed** the bushes.         _____
12. Dad **cut** a small tree.           _____

## H3. Ask questions.

1. Sara **watered** the flowers.        *Did Sara **water** the flowers?*
2. He **chose** fruit for dessert.      _____
3. They **did** their homework.         _____
4. Dad **mowed** the lawn.              _____
5. His son **bet** ten dollars.         _____
6. Mom **pulled** the weeds.            _____
7. A strong wind **blew** at noon.      _____
8. We **bought** two spades.            _____
9. Greg **bent** the handle.            _____
10. Ray **used** the shears.            _____
11. Edward **brought** two picks.       _____

## H4.  Answer the questions.

1.  Did mom **water** the plants?

*Yes,* she *watered* the plants.
*No,* she *didn't water* the plants

2.  Did Charles **mow** the lawn?

_____
_____

3.  Did Henry **dig** any holes?

_____

4.  Did you **bring** any tools?

_____

5.  Did Carol **bet** any money?

_____

6.  Did the man **break** the pick?

_____

7.  Did he **buy** another one?

_____

8.  Did Henry **pull** the weeds?

_____

9.  Did the two boys **help**?

_____

10.  Did they **do** any work?

_____

11.  Did they **weigh** the bags?

_____

12.  Did they **cut** any roses?

_____

13.  Did they **pick up** the trash?

_____

**H5.** Change *every Saturday* for *last Saturday.*

**Every Saturday,** my oldest son Charles **is** in charge of maintaining the garden neat and clean. He **starts** to work in the garden early. First of all, he **trims** the bushes and the trees. Then he **plants** trees and plants. He **purchases** the plants from the nursery.

Afterwards he **pulls** the weeds. He **uses** a light hoe and a heavy pick. When he **finishes** pulling the weeds, he **picks up** the leaves from the ground. He **puts** the trash in plastic bags. The black garden bags are the biggest of all.

**Every Saturday,** Chuck **fills** three plastic bags with trash. Each one **weighs** forty-five pounds.

*Last Saturday* _____

_____

_____

_____

_____

_____

_____

_____

_____

_____

_____

_____

_____

_____

_____

_____

_____

_____

_____

# Lesson #3

## The Farm

## Index

### Audio & Translations

English Audio available online for sections A-E.

Translations in various Languages available online for Sections A, B, and E.

**www.BasicESL.com**

**1.** field

**2.** farmer

**3.** haystack

**4.** fence

**5.** herd

**6.** swine

**7.** cattle

**8.** crop

**9.** stable

**10.** barn

**11.** tractor

**12.** to feed

**13.** to till

**14.** to plow

**15.** to sow

**16.** to harvest

**17.** to fertilize

**18.** to irrigate

## Vocabulary Study: Other Vocabulary

| | | | | | | |
|---|---|---|---|---|---|---|
| 1. | n | crop | 12. | v | get back (got) |
| 2. | n | farmer | 13. | v | head |
| 3. | n | fear | 14. | v | increase |
| 4. | n | field | 15. | v | notice |
| 5. | n | forest | 16. | v | ride (rode) |
| 6. | n | land | 17. | v | roam |
| 7. | n | property | 18. | v | surround |
| 8. | n | sand | 19. | v | take (took) |
| 9. | n | trail | 20. | v | trail |
| 10. | n | variety | 21. | v | wind |
| 11. | adj | winding | 22. | adv | by the time |

For the audio pronunciations and written translations of **Sections A and B,** please go to:

# www.basicesl.com

## Vocabulary Study: Other Vocabulary

| | | | | | | |
|---|---|---|---|---|---|---|
| 1. | n | back | 11. | v | eat (ate) |
| 2. | n | edge | 12. | v | embrace |
| 3. | n | equipment | 13. | v | feed (fed) |
| 4. | n | farm | 14. | v | lead (led) |
| 5. | n | fine | 15. | v | plow |
| 6. | n | harvest | 16. | v | see (saw) |
| 7. | n | job | 17. | v | sow |
| 8. | n | seed | 18. | v | spend time |
| 9. | n | tool | 19. | v | take care |
| 10. | n | tractor | 20. | adv | during |

## B1. Modal Verb: "may, might"

| | |
|---|---|
| **(request)** | **May** I walk to the countryside?<br>**May** I bathe in the stream? |
| **(possibility)** | He cannot do that today.<br>He **might** do that tomorrow. |
| **(probability)** | Ann is going on an excursion.<br>Carol **may** accompany her. |
| **(wish)** | **May** God **bless** you!<br>**May** you **have** a safe trip. |

## B2. "may, might": Affirmative Sentences

I **may** clean the barn today.
She **might** clean the stable later.

Tom **may** climb the hill.
Joe **might** climb with Tom.

We **may** plow the land this year.
We **might** plant trees next year.

The boys **may** prepare the tent.
They **might** sleep there today.

## B3. "may, might": Negative Sentences

Dad **may not** sell the cattle now.
He **might** do it later.

I **may not** walk to the field today.
I **might** do it next week.

She **may not** go camping now.
She **might** do it in two days.

We **may not** trim the bushes now.
We **might** do it next month.

### B1 - B2 - B3

*Modal* or *auxiliary* verbs are those verbs used to express different attitudes of the subject regarding the action of the verb. These attitudes of the subject can indicate: obligation, permission, advise, necessity, or probability.

*The verb "may"* (present) and *"might"* (past) indicate permission, request, possibility, probability or desire. They are followed by the main verb without "to."

*Negative sentences* with modal verbs are formed with "*not*" following the modal verb.

## B4. "may, might": Short Answers

**ⓘ**

*May I look at the scenery today?*
Yes, you **may** look at the scenery.
Yes, you **may**.

*May I sit by the fire?*
No, you **may not** sit by the fire.
No, you **may not**.

*May they start the harvest?*
No, they **may not** start the harvest.
No, they **may not**.

**B4**

*Questions* with *modal verbs begin* with the modal verb followed by the subject.

*Short answers with modal verbs are formed by repeating the modal verb in the answer.*

## B5. List of irregular Verbs

*What did you catch at the lake?*
I **caught** a big fish.

*What language did they choose?*
They **chose** Spanish.

*Did you come late?*
Yes, I **came** five minutes late.

*Did the man hurt Charles?*
Yes, he **hurt** Charles.

## B6. List of irregular Verbs

*What did you grow in the garden?*
I **grew** all kinds of vegetables.

*How much did the tractor cost?*
It **cost** $10,000.

*Did your nose bleed a lot?*
Yes, it **bled** a lot.

*Where did they cling?*
They **clung** to a bush.

## C1. Read and Listen to the story.

I enjoy taking long road trips. My sister and I took a nice trip last month. We traveled from Indiana to Tennessee by car. We started our trip in Indiana. We ate lunch in the sand next to Lake Michigan. There were lots of hiking trails in the park and many families were swimming in the lake.

Once we got back on the road, we headed towards Kentucky. When we arrived in Kentucky we saw beautiful fields of grass. We passed by many farm houses with animals roaming around. There were many long winding roads in Kentucky. We even saw a few people riding brown horses. By the time we reached Tennessee we noticed a lot of gorgeous forest. The trees were changing colors. We had a great time on our trip. I hope we may repeat the same trip in a couple of months.

## C2. Read and Listen to the story.

My brother-in-law is a cabbage farmer. I am spending the summer with him. He is teaching me how to farm. His farm is very large. He has a lot of land but few animals. When you arrive to the farm, there is a driveway leading to a barn in the back of the property. The barn is filled with lots of farm equipment. He has a huge tractor and tools that he uses to plow the ground.

During the summer he harvests the cabbage crop. At the same time he grows many other vegetables. When you look across the field, there is a variety of colors from all different vegetables that are growing. My brother-in-law has a goat, and a few chickens. He might bring two pigs this year. It is my job to feed the animals while he takes care of the vegetable garden.

**D1.** parents / to grow

**Do your parents grow onions?**
They grew onions last year.

**Are they going to grow onions this year?**
They may not grow onions this year.

**How about next year?**
They might grow onions again.

**D2.** brother / to feed

**Does your brother feed the animals?**
He fed the animals last year.

**Is he going to feed the animals this year?**
He may not feed the animals this year.

**How about next year?**
He might feed the animals again.

**D3.** they / to plow

**Do they plow the land?**
They plowed the land last year.

**Are they going to plow the land this year?**
They may not plow the land this year.

**How about next year?**
They might plow the land again.

**D4.** Cynthia / to dig

**Does Cynthia dig holes?**
She dug holes last year.

**Is she going to dig holes this year?**
She might not dig holes this year.

**How about next year?**
She might dig holes again.

## Verb "to get"

1. How do you **get by?**
2. How do you **get in** without the key?
3. I **get off** the bus in downtown.
4. Tony, **get down** from the roof.
5. **Get out** of my house right now.
6. He **got away.**
7. **Get back** to school now.
8. It is hard to **get over** this.
9. I **got** this **across** Paul.
10. What time do you **get up**?

**Phrasal verbs** or **prepositional verbs** are verbs followed by a preposition or an adverb. When the verb is followed by a preposition or adverb, the verb acquires a different meaning from the original meaning. When the object of the phrasal verb is a direct object pronoun, the pronoun is placed between the verb and the preposition.

For the English audio pronunciations and written native language translations of **section E,** please go to:

## www.basicesl.com

**Get out** of the house.

It's hard to **get over** this.

End of the **oral exercises** for lesson 3.

**You can find additional exercises in sections D, F & G at Basic ESL Online.**

Please continue with the **written exercises** for this lesson in **section H.**

Lesson
**3**

## H1. Write these irregular verbs in the past tense.

1. bear    _____
2. beat    _____
3. become    _____
4. begin    _____
5. cost    _____
6. bleed    _____
7. bite    _____
8. grow    _____

cling    _____
catch    _____
dig    _____
feed    _____
burst    _____
break    _____
bring    _____
buy    _____

## H2. Ask the question corresponding to these answers.

1. He brought some **plants.**     *What did he bring?*
2. The dog bit **the child**.    _____
3. They bought **2** tractors.    _____
4. The tractors were **big**?    _____
5. He plowed the land with **a pick**.    _____
6. Lydia began to work **early**.    _____
7. **Nancy** grew lots of onions.    _____
8. The onions tasted **very good**.    _____

## H3. Make the sentences negative.

1. You **walk** early to the field.  *You **don't walk** early to the field.*
2. Fred **can** plow the land.  _____
3. Carol **walked** home late.  _____
4. I **may** see you tomorrow.  _____
5. Tony **dug** three holes.  _____
6. He **likes** to work in the garden.  _____
7. My brother **fed** the animals.  _____
8. I **am feeding** the animals today.  _____
9. They **might** sell the barn.  _____
10. She **could** remember you.  _____
11. Jenifer **sowed** the seeds.  _____
12. **He is** tilling the land now.  _____

## H4. Ask questions.

1. You **walk** early to the field.  *Do you **walk** early to the field?*
2. Fred **can** plow the land.  _____
3. Carol **walked** home late.  _____
4. I **may** see you tomorrow.  _____
5. Tony **dug** three holes.  _____
6. He **likes** to work in the garden.  _____
7. My brother **fed** the animals.  _____
8. I **am feeding** the animals today.  _____
9. They **might** sell the barn.  _____
10. She **could** remember you.  _____
11. She **may** go home now.  _____

## H5. Answer the questions with short answers.

1. **Did** you **feed** the animals?     *Yes, I did.*     *No, I didn't.*

2. **Are** the animals free? _____ _____

3. **Can** they leave the farm? _____ _____

4. **May** your dad sell the farm? _____ _____

5. **Does** Mary own some cows? _____ _____

6. **Could** she buy more cows? _____ _____

7. **Is** she **going** to buy more cows? _____ _____

8. **Might** she change her mind? _____ _____

9. **Did** she do that last time? _____ _____

10. **Are** you sure this time? _____ _____

## H6. Make comparisons using adjectives.

1. My pen costs $4.50. Yours costs $3.50.

   ***My pen is more expensive than yours.***

2. John weighs 130 pounds. Ann weighs 125 pounds.

   _____

3. We're 12 years old. Lisa is 12 years old also.

   _____

4. My desk is 36"wide. Yours is 25" wide.

   _____

5. This book is 1" thick. That one is 2" thick.

   _____

6. My pool is 6' deep. The river is only 1' deep.

   _____

## H7. Select the correct answer

| 1. A plant with thorns | palm tree | tulip | juniper | rose |
| 2. A red flower | daisy | rose | fern | tree |
| 3. Which has branches? | lily | carnation | oak tree | violet |
| 4. A desert plant | ivy | cactus | olive tree | magnolia |
| 5. I dig holes with a …. | rake | pick | fork | hose |
| 6. A plant with petals | bamboo | pine tree | sugar cane | tulip |
| 7. The widest part of a tree | leaf | branch | root | trunk |

## H8. Multiple choice.

1. Yesterday Henry _____ out the weeds.          pull, pulls, *pulled*

2. Every day he _____ the flowers.          water, waters, watering

3. _____ I dig holes tomorrow?          did, may, does

4. My brother _____ picks and shovels.          buy, digs, uses

5. I did not _____ any rake.          brought, bring, bought

6. Alex _____ up the trash today.          picks, picked, is picking

7. Rick is _____ than Andy.          tall, taller, the tallest

8. Rick is _____ of all the students.          tall, taller, the tallest

9. Henry is _____ young as you.          young, younger, as young

10. Paul is _____ than you.          young, younger, as young

11. He is not younger _____ Carol.          in, than, of

12. A rose is prettier _____ a fern.          as, than, in

13. Tulips are the prettiest flowers _____ all.          at, of, in

14. Mom _____ many flowers last year.          don't grow, grew, is growing

# Chapter 2
# The Human Body

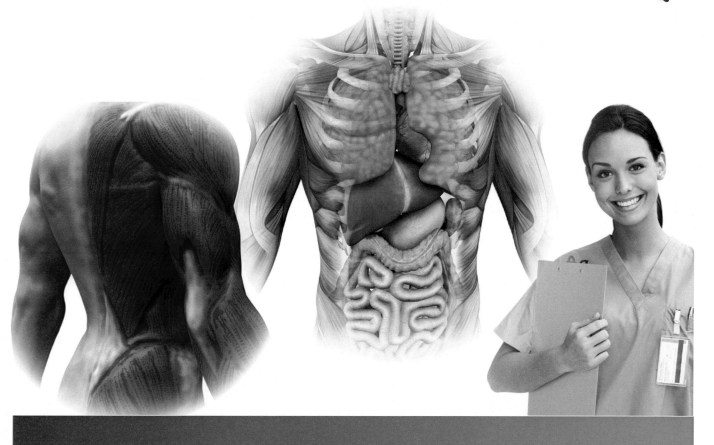

Lesson 4:   Parts of the Body
Lesson 5:   Body Organs
Lesson 6:   Illnesses

# What to do in each section of every lesson...

## A - Vocabulary Study

Section A includes the vocabulary that will be used throughout the lesson. Learning new vocabulary is basic to learning a new language.

**Read** the vocabulary several times.
If you are on Basic ESL Online:
**Listen** to the **English audio pronunciation**.
**View** the **native language translations** of the vocabulary.

Listen and read the vocabulary until you can understand the vocabulary without looking at the words.

## B - Sentence Structure

Section B teaches students basic English sentences using the vocabulary in section A.

**Read** and **study** the sentences.
If you are on Basic ESL Online:
**Listen** to the **English audio pronunciation**.
**View** the **native language translations** of the sentences.
**View** the **grammar concepts** by clicking on the **information button** [i] .

Repeat the sentences as many times as needed. Continue to the next section once you can **understand** the sentences without looking at them.

## C - Listening Exercises

**Read** the story or dialog several times.
If you are on Basic ESL Online, **listen** to the story or dialog while reading it several times.

Once you are familiar with the story or dialog, try to see if you can **understand** it by only listening without reading.

## D - Conversation Exercises

**Read** the conversation dialogs several times.
If you are on Basic ESL Online, **listen** to the dialogs until you can understand them without looking at them.

Finally, try to **speak** the conversation dialogs by only looking at the pictures and key words.

## E - Common Phrases

Many of the **common phrases** that are presented in this section are frequently used by the native English speakers in their everyday life.

**Read** the common phrases several times.
If you are on Basic ESL Online, **listen** to the common phrases while reading. **Listen** as many times as needed until you can understand the common phrases without looking at the sentences.

## H - Written Exercises

The written exercises provide an opportunity to test what you learned in the lesson. You can never be sure of knowing something unless you can put it in writing.

You can check your answers by going to the **Answer Key Section** in the back of the workbook.

For information regarding **Basic ESL Online,** please visit **www.basicesl.com**.
🎧Audio Pronunciaton of English & 🌐Native Language Translations.

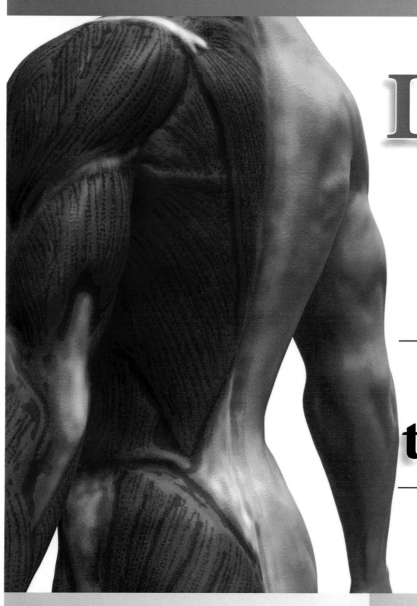

# Lesson #4

## Parts of the Body

## Index

## Audio & Translations

English Audio available online for sections A-E.

Translations in various Languages available online for Sections A, B, and E.

**www.BasicESL.com**

**1.** head

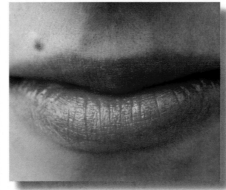
**2.** mouth

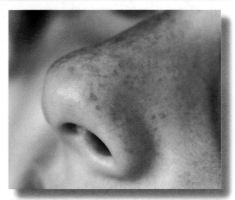
**3.** nose

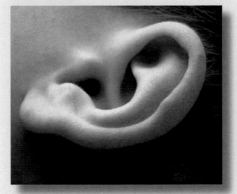
**4.** ear

**5.** hair

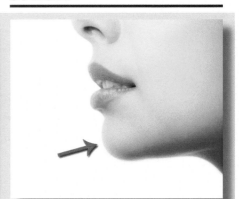
**6.** chin

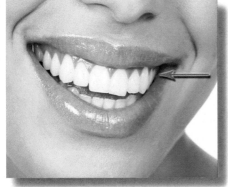
**7.** teeth

**8.** face

**9.** eye

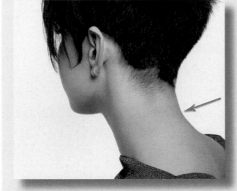
**10.** neck

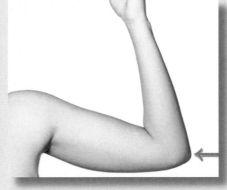
**11.** elbow

**12.** shoulder

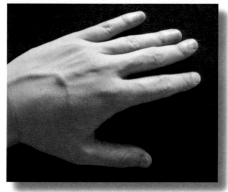

**13.** hand

**14.** arm

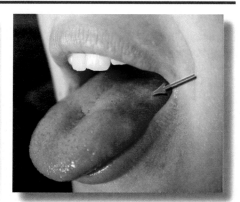

**15.** tongue

**16.** wrist

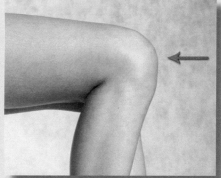

**17.** knee

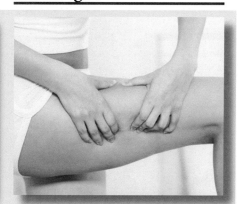

**18.** thigh

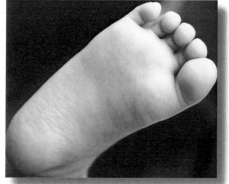

**19.** foot

**20.** finger

**21.** leg

**22.** hip

**23.** chest

**24.** back

## Vocabulary Study: Other Vocabulary

| | | |
|---|---|---|
| 1. | n | air |
| 2. | n | brain |
| 3. | n | lips |
| 4. | n | function |
| 5. | n | passage |
| 6. | n | purpose |
| 7. | n | skin |
| 8. | n | skull |
| 9. | adj | upper |
| 10. | v | breathe |

| | | |
|---|---|---|
| 11. | v | chew |
| 12. | v | distinguish |
| 13. | v | grind |
| 14. | v | include |
| 15. | v | kick |
| 16. | v | kiss |
| 17. | v | move |
| 18. | v | smell |
| 19. | v | support |
| 20. | v | swallow |

For the audio pronunciations and written translations of **Sections A and B,** please go to:

**www.basicesl.com**

## Vocabulary Study: Other Vocabulary

| | | |
|---|---|---|
| 1. | n | dizziness |
| 2. | n | illness |
| 3. | n | injection |
| 4. | n | operation |
| 5. | n | shot |
| 6. | n | sickness |
| 7. | n | whistling |
| 8. | adj | bruised |
| 9. | adj | constant |
| 10. | adj | dizzy |

| | | |
|---|---|---|
| 11. | adj | ill |
| 12. | adj | normal |
| 13. | adj | painful |
| 14. | adj | sick |
| 15. | adj | sore |
| 16. | v | inject |
| 17. | v | sneeze |
| 18. | v | sooth |
| 19. | v | throw up |
| 20. | v | vomit |

## B1. Singular Nouns: Possessive Form (PF)

|  | The mouth **of John** is big. |
| PF | **John's** mouth is big. |
|  | The eyes **of Mike** are infected. |
| PF | **Mike's** eyes are infected. |
|  | The hair **of Mary** is blond. |
| PF | **Mary's** hair is blond. |
|  | The neck **of the girl** is stiff. |
| PF | The **girl's** neck is stiff. |

## B2. Plural Nounts: Possessive Form

|  | The hands **of the boys** are cured. |
| PF | The **boys'** hands are cured. |
|  | The teeth **of the girls** are white. |
| PF | The **girls'** teeth are white. |
|  | The ears **of my nieces** are plugged. |
| PF | My **nieces'** ears are plugged. |
|  | The legs **of my uncles** are swollen. |
| PF | My **uncles'** legs are swollen. |

## B3. Irregular Plural Nouns: Possessive Form (PF)

|  | The father **of the child** is rich. |
| PF | The **child's** father is rich. |
|  | The mother **of the children** is nice. |
| PF | The **children's** mother is nice. |
|  | The clothes **of the men** are red. |
| PF | The **men's** clothes are red. |
|  | The clothes **of the women** are black. |
| PF | The **women's** clothes are black. |

### B1 - B2 - B3

In English, **possession** is expressed in two ways:

1. with the preposition **"of"**

2. with the **possessive form** of the noun, which is formed with an **apostrophe plus an s ('s)** after the singular noun.

With plural nouns the possessive form is formed **only** with the **apostrophe (')**.

With nouns having an **irregular plural form**, the **possessive form** is formed with the **('s)** after the irregular singular or plural noun.

## B4. Question Word: "whose"

(Helen)
*Whose lips are these?*
They are **Helen's** lips.

(Andy)
*Whose children are these?*
They are **Andy's** children.

(teacher)
*Whose book is that?*
It is **the teacher's** book.

(sons)
*Whose shoes are those?*
They are **my sons'** shoes.

**B4**

*The question word "**whose**" is used to obtain information about the identity of the owner.*

## B5. List of Irregular Verbs

(John)
*Whose car **did** you **drive?***
I **drove** John's car.

(you)
*Whose coffee **did** you **drink?***
I **drank** your coffee. I'm sorry.

(sister)
*Whose picture **did** you **draw?***
I **drew** my sister's picture.

(mom)
*Whose food **did** you **eat?***
I **ate** my mom's food.

## B6. List of Irregular Verbs

*Where **did** your aunt **fall?***
She **fell** in the bathroom.

***Did** you **hear** the latest news?*
Yes, I **heard** the latest news.

***Did** you **feed** the children?*
Yes, I **fed** the children.

*How **did** you **feel** yesterday?*
I **felt** very good.

## C1. Read and Listen to the Story.

The human body consists of the head, the neck, the torso, the arms, and the legs. The **head** is the upper part of the body. It consists of the face the skull and the brain. The face includes the skin, the hair, the eyes, the lashes, the nose, the ears, the lips, and the mouth. Inside the mouth we find the tongue and the teeth. The face is what distinguishes one person from another. Parts of the face are also the chin and the jaw.

The **neck** is the part of the body that supports the head. It joins the head with the shoulders. In the neck we find the throat. The throat is the passage thru which air and food keeps our body alive. The **arm** consists of the shoulder, the elbow, the wrist, the hand and the fingers. The **leg** includes the hip, the thigh, the knee, the ankle, the foot and the toes.

## C2. Read and Listen to the dialog.

**What's the function of the eyes?**
We can see with our eyes.

**What do we do with the tongue?**
We swallow the food.

**What is the purpose of the ears?**
We listen and hear with our ears.

**What are the lips for?**
We kiss with the lips.

**What do we do with the nose?**
We smell through the nose.

**What's the function of the neck?**
Its function is to move the head.

**What do you do with the mouth?**
We speak and eat with the mouth.

**What is the purpose of the throat?**
We breathe through the throat.

**What is the purpose of the teeth?**
It is to chew and grind the food.

**What do we do with the feet?**
We run and kick with the feet.

**D1.** Carol (smell) / breath

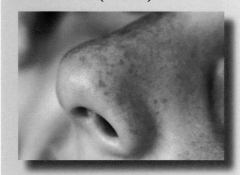

*Whose nose is this?*
    It is **Carol's** nose.

*What does she do with **her** nose?*
    She smells with **her** nose.

*What else does she do?*
    She can **breath** through **her** nose.

**D2.** Paul (catch) / write

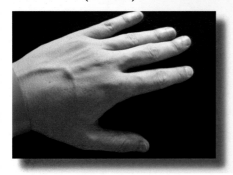

*Whose hand is it?*
    It is **Paul's** hand.

*What does he do with **his** hands?*
    He **catches** things with **his** hands.

*What else can he do?*
    He can **write** with **his** hands.

**D3.** Jan (chew) / bite

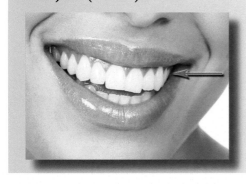

*Whose teeth are these?*
    They are **Jan's** teeth.

*What does she do with **her** teeth?*
    She **chews** with **her** teeth.

*What else can she do with **her** teeth?*
    She can **bite** with **her** teeth.

**D4.** brother (walk) / kick

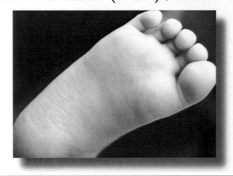

*Whose foot is this?*
    It is my **brother's** foot.

*What does he do with **his** feet?*
    He **walks** with **his** feet.

*What else can he do with **his** feet?*
    He can **kick** with **his** feet.

## Verb "to get"

1. I don't **get along** with Jennifer.
2. What are you **getting at**?
3. Why don't we **get together**?
4. The car **got across** suddenly.

## Verb "to give"

1. Don't **give up** so soon.
2. She **gave away** everything.
3. She **gave me back** the letters.
4. We **gave in** to his terms.
5. **Give way** to the ladies.

**Phrasal verbs** or **prepositional verbs** are verbs followed by a preposition or an adverb. When the verb is followed by a preposition or adverb, the verb acquires a different meaning from the original meaning. When the object of the phrasal verb is a direct object pronoun, the pronoun is placed between the verb and the preposition.

For the English audio pronunciations and written native language translations of **section E,** please go to:

# www.basicesl.com

Don't **give up** so soon.

I don't **get along** with Jennifer.

End of the **oral exercises** for lesson 4.

**You can find additional exercises in sections D, F & G at Basic ESL Online.**

Please continue with the **written exercises** for this lesson in **section H.**

**Lesson**

**4**

## H1. Write the past tense of these verbs.

| | | | | |
|---|---|---|---|---|
| 1. | drive | _____ | build | _____ |
| 2. | drink | _____ | grind | _____ |
| 3. | draw | _____ | cut | _____ |
| 4. | eat | _____ | blow | _____ |
| 5. | fall | _____ | break | _____ |
| 6. | hear | _____ | bend | _____ |
| 7. | feed | _____ | bring | _____ |
| 8. | feel | _____ | bleed | _____ |

## H2. Use the possessive form of the noun.

1. the eyes of the boy     *The **boy's** eyes.*

2. the eyes of the boys     _____

3. the eyes of Mary     _____

4. the hand of Fred     _____

5. the hands of the man     _____

6. the hands of the men     _____

7. the hands of the girls     _____

8. the head of Carol     _____

## H3. Change to the possessive form of the noun.

1. The hand **of the child** is infected.  |  *The **child's hand** is infected.*

2. The leg **of Paul** is getting better.  |  _____

3. The teeth **of my uncle** are yellow.  |  _____

4. The ears **of Liz** are plugged.  |  _____

5. The neck **of the man** is stiff.  |  _____

6. I like the hair **of Jane**.  |  _____

7. The hats **of the women** are blue.  |  _____

8. The tongue **of Ann** is white.  |  _____

9. The clothes **of Joe** are expensive.  |  _____

10. The feet **of the boys** are dirty.  |  _____

## H4. Answer using the subject in (...).

1. Whose lips **are** they?  (*Margaret*)
   ***They are Margaret's lips.***

2. Whose car **are** you **driving**? (*father*)

   _____

3. Whose face **did** you **draw** while you were at school? (*Jenifer*)

   _____

4. Whose medicine **did** Tony **drink** at home? (*sister*)

   _____

5. Whose food **did** the dog **eat** last night? (*baby*)

   _____

6. Whose pills **did** the children **swallow**? (*aunt*)

   _____

7. Whose house **did** the city **build**? (*teacher*)

   _____

## H5. Follow the example.

1.      sister / kiss

**lips**

**Whose lips are these?**

*They are my sister's lips.*

*She kisses with her lips.*

2.      girls / smell

**noses**

_____

_____

_____

3.      woman / see

**eye**

_____

_____

_____

4.      women / hear

**ears**

_____

_____

_____

5.      Tom / walk

**foot**

_____

_____

_____

**H6.** Answer the questions.

The **head** is the upper part of the body. In the head we find the hair and the face.

The **face** includes the skin, the eyes, the lashes, the nose, the ears, the lips and the mouth. Inside the mouth we find the tongue and the teeth. The face is what distinguishes one person from another. Parts of the face are also the chin and the jaw.

The **neck** is the part of the body that supports the head. It joins the head with the shoulders. In the neck we find the throat.

The **arm** consists of the shoulder, the elbow, the wrist, the hand and the fingers. The **leg** includes the hip, the thigh, the knee, the ankle, the foot and the toes.

1. *What do we find in the head?*

_____

2. *Are the eyes part of the face?*

_____

3. *Are the lips above the nose or below the nose?*

_____

4. *Where is the tongue located?*

_____

5. *Does the chin belong to the neck?*

_____

6. *What is the function of the neck?*

_____

_____

7. *Is the shoulder or the throat part of the neck?*

_____

_____

8. *What do we use to pick up objects?*

_____

9. *Does the leg include the elbow?*

_____

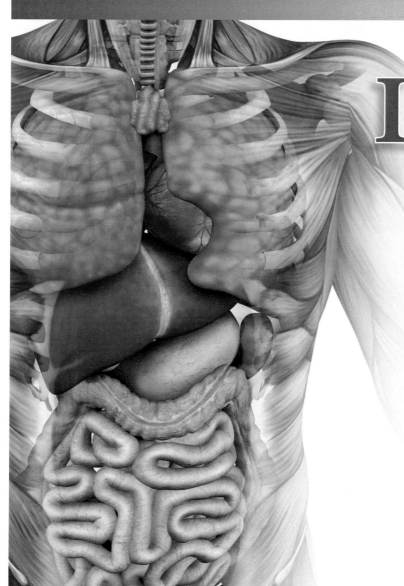

# Lesson #5

## Body Organs

## Audio & Translations

**English Audio available online for sections A-E.**

**Translations in various Languages available online for Sections A, B, and E.**

**www.BasicESL.com**

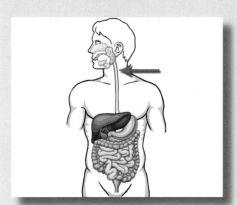

**1.** throat

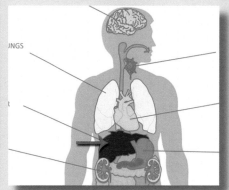

**2.** liver

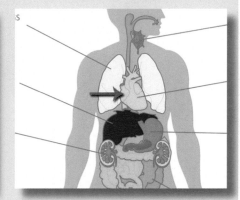

**3.** heart

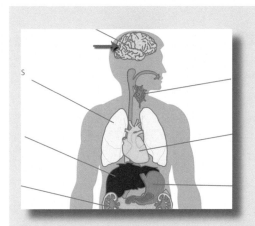

**4.** brain

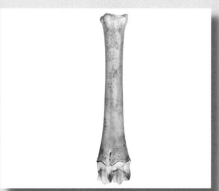

**5.** bone

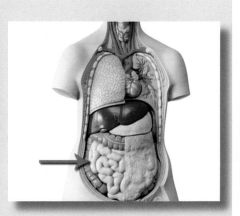

**6.** bowels

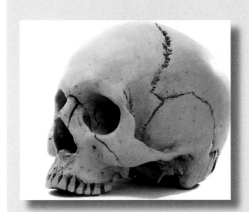

**7.** skull

**8.** stomach

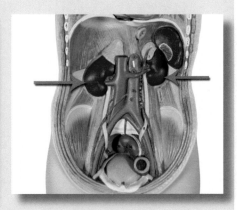

**9.** kidneys

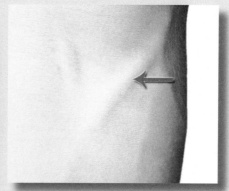

**10.** lungs

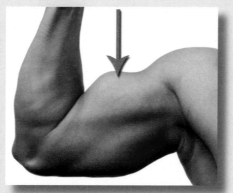

**11.** muscles

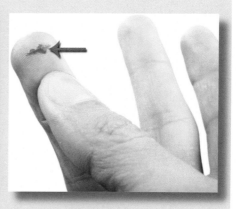

**12.** vein

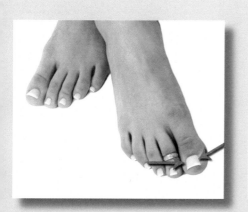

**13.** toenail

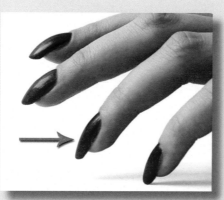

**14.** fingernail

**15.** blood

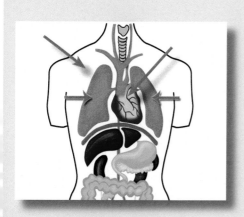

**16.** rib

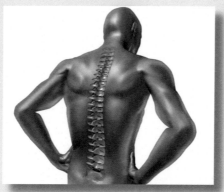

**17.** spine

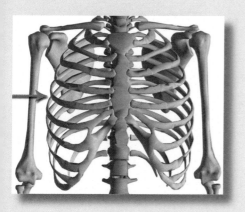

**18.** skeleton

## Vocabulary Study: Other Vocabulary

| | | | | | |
|---|---|---|---|---|---|
| 1. | n | appointment | 12. | n | symptom |
| 2. | n | check-up | 13. | n | temperature |
| 3. | n | examination | 14. | v | tell (told) |
| 4. | n | fever | 15. | v | fill |
| 5. | n | medication | 16. | v | run a test (ran) |
| 6. | n | pharmacy | 17. | v | set |
| 7. | n | pressure | 18. | v | take (took) |
| 8. | n | side | 19. | v | go (went) |
| 9. | n | side effects | 20. | con | therefore |
| 10. | n | sore | 21. | pre | according to |
| 11. | n | stomach ache | 22. | adv | immediately |

For the audio pronunciations and written translations of **Sections A and B,** please go to:

# www.basicesl.com

## Vocabulary Study: Other Vocabulary

| | | | | | |
|---|---|---|---|---|---|
| 1. | n | antibiotics | 12. | v | have (had) |
| 2. | n | congestion | 13. | v | hold |
| 3. | n | dosage | 14. | v | hurt (hurt) |
| 4. | n | infection | 15. | v | produce |
| 5. | n | phlegm | 16. | v | pull up |
| 6. | n | pill | 17. | v | shiver |
| 7. | n | runny nose | 18. | v | skip |
| 8. | adj | mild | 19. | v | stick out |
| 9. | v | breathe | 20. | v | whistle |
| 10. | v | check | 21. | adv | how long |
| 11. | v | cough | 22. | v | check |

## B1. Modal Verb: "should"

**i**

I **should** stretch my muscles.
I **should not** stretch my fingers.
I **shouldn't** stretch my fingers.

You **should** check your lungs.
You **should not** check your feet.
You **shouldn't** check your feet.

They **should** clean their stomach.
They **should not** clean their ears.
They **shouldn't** clean their ears.

## B2. "Should" and "Ought to"

**i**

I **should** strengthen my bones.
I **ought to** strengthen my bones.

You **should** clean your fingernails.
You **ought to** clean your fingernails.

They **should not** forget that.
They **ought not to** forget that.

She **should not** touch her eyes.
She **ought not to** touch her eyes.

## B3. "Should": Questions and Answers

**i**

**Should** I take this pill?
  Yes, you **should.**
  No, you **shouldn't.**

**Should** Tom cut his fingernails?
  Yes, he **should.**
  No, he **shouldn't.**

**Should** Ann polish her toenails?
  Yes, she **should.**
  No, she **shouldn't.**

### B1 - B2

*"Should"* is used to give or ask for **advise**. Its equivalent is the modal verb *"ought to."*

Negative sentences with the verb *"should"* or *"ought to"* are formed with the word *"not"* after the modal verbs. *"Should not"* can be contracted to *"shouldn't."*

### B3

*"Should"* is used in at the beginning of questions. In this case, the subject is offering or asking for advice.

## B4. Noun Adjectives (NA)

The school **of John** is big.
**John's** school is big.

The door **of the house** is green.
NA   The **house** door is green.

I like the car **of my sister**.
I like **my sister's** car.

We like the color **of the room**.
NA   We like the **room** color.

## B5. List of Irregular Verbs

Where **did** they **find** Rudy?
   They **found** Rudy under the bridge.

**Did** the doctor **forbid** Paul to play?
   Yes, he **forbade** Paul to play.

**Did** you **forget** your own age?
   Yes, I **forgot** my own age.

**Did** you **fly** to Argentina?
   Yes, I **flew** there last year.

## B6. List of Irregular Verbs

**Did** they **forecast** the two wars?
Yes, they **forecast** both wars.

Why **did** he **flee** from the jail?
He **fled** because he was afraid.

**Did** the refrigerator **freeze** the fruit?
Yes, it **froze** the fruit.

**Did** Fred **forgive** his son?
Yes, he **forgave** his son.

## C1. Read and Listen to the Story.

Last week I had a sore throat and a stomach ache. I called the doctor and set an appointment for a checkup. When I arrived at the clinic, the nurse weighed me and asked me about my symptoms. She also took my temperature and my blood pressure. Then she led me to the doctor's office for my examination.

The doctor said that I had a fever. He ran a couple of tests and prescribed some medication. He told me to rest for a couple of days. The doctor said that the medication may have some side effects. Therefore, I should not drive my car while taking the medication. I immediately went to the pharmacy and had the prescription filled. According to the doctor, I should feel better soon. If not, I should return to the clinic again.

## C2. Read and Listen to the dialog.

*Hello, I am Dr. Ryan.*
Good morning, doctor.

*What is wrong?*
I have a runny nose.

*Do you have a cough also?*
I am coughing constantly.

*When did the cough start?*
It started a week ago.

*Is it a dry cough?*
No, it produces a phlegm.

*What color is the phlegm?*
It is kind of brown.

*Do you feel any fever?*
Yes, I do.

*Do you feel any shivering?*
No, I don't.

*Let me see your throat.*

*Open your mouth.*

*Stick out your tongue.*

*Your throat is a little sore.*

**D1.** Mary (pain) / back (hurt)

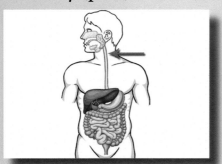

**What is wrong with Mary?**
　　She feels pain in her throat.

**Does her back hurt too?**
　　Yes, it does.

**Shouldn't she go to the doctor?**
　　Yes, she should.
　　The sooner the better.

**D2.** Rose (pain) / lung (hurt)

**What is wrong with Rose?**
　　She feels pain in her stomach.

**Do her lungs hurt too?**
　　Yes, they do.

**Shouldn't she go to the doctor?**
　　Yes, she should.
　　The sooner the better

**D3.** brothers (pain) / leg (hurt)

**What is wrong with your brothers?**
　　They feel pain in their arms.

**Do their legs hurt too?**
　　Yes, they do.

**Shouldn't they go to the doctor?**
　　Yes, they should.
　　The sooner the better.

**D4.** uncle (pain) / bone (hurt)

**What is wrong with the uncle?**
　　He feels pain in his chest.

**Do his bones hurt also?**
　　Yes, they do.

**Shouldn't he go to the doctor?**
　　Yes, he should.
　　The sooner the better.

## Verb "to pass"

1. **I passed out** at the hospital.
2. My uncle **passed away** yesterday.
3. The church **passed around** the bread.

## Verb "to pay"

1. He refuses to **pay back** the money.
2. Today I **pay off** the loan.
3. It **pays off** to be good.

## Verb "to pick"

1. He is always **picking on** me.
2. **Pick up** the paper from the floor.
3. Mary, **pick up** the phone, please.

**Phrasal verbs** or **prepositional verbs** are verbs followed by a preposition or an adverb. When the verb is followed by a preposition or adverb, the verb acquires a different meaning from the original meaning. When the object of the phrasal verb is a direct object pronoun, the pronoun is placed between the verb and the preposition.

For the English audio pronunciations and written native language translations of **section E,** please go to:

## www.basicesl.com

Today I **pay off** the loan.

It **pays off** to be good.

End of the **oral exercises** for lesson 5.

**You can find additional exercises in sections D, F & G at Basic ESL Online.**

Please continue with the **written exercises** for this lesson in **section H.**

Lesson
# 5

## H1. Write the past tense of these verbs.

| | | | |
|---|---|---|---|
| 1. find | _____ | drive | _____ |
| 2. forbid | _____ | drink | _____ |
| 3. forget | _____ | draw | _____ |
| 4. fly | _____ | eat | _____ |
| 5. forecast | _____ | fall | _____ |
| 6. flee | _____ | hear | _____ |
| 7. freeze | _____ | feed | _____ |
| 8. forgive | _____ | feel | _____ |

## H2. Change *should* for its equivalent.

1. You **should** clean your neck.     *You **ought to** clean your neck.*
2. They should cut their nails.     _____
3. She should stretch her legs.     _____
4. He should stop the bleeding.     _____
5. Tom should check his lungs.     _____
6. I should polish my toenails.     _____
7. We should strengthen the bones.     _____
8. You should clear the throat.     _____

## H3. Make the sentences negative.

| | | |
|---|---|---|
| 1. | Cindy **forgot** your address. | *Cindy **did not forget** your address.* |
| 2. | You **should** see your cousin. | _____ |
| 3. | Mary **forgave** her nephews. | _____ |
| 4. | I **ought to** eat more. | _____ |
| 5. | I **can** walk far. | _____ |
| 6. | Henry **called** Liz yesterday. | _____ |
| 7. | She **felt** some pain. | _____ |
| 8. | The boys **were** are home. | _____ |
| 9. | The doctor **flew** to Canada. | _____ |
| 10. | He **may** return soon. | _____ |
| 11. | He **goes** there often. | _____ |
| 12. | I **froze** the juice. | _____ |

## H4. Change the statments to questions.

| | | |
|---|---|---|
| 1. | Cindy **forgot** your address. | *Did Cindy **forget** your address?* |
| 2. | I **should** see your cousin. | _____ |
| 3. | Mary **forgave** her nephews. | _____ |
| 4. | Fred **has to** eat more. | _____ |
| 5. | I **can** walk far. | _____ |
| 6. | Henry **called** Liz yesterday. | _____ |
| 7. | She **felt** some pain. | _____ |
| 8. | The boys **were** at home. | _____ |
| 9. | The doctor **flew** to Canada. | _____ |
| 10. | He **may** return soon. | _____ |
| 11. | He **goes** there often. | _____ |
| 12. | I **froze** the juice. | _____ |

## H5. Answer the questions with short answers.

1. **Are** you going to the hospital?     *Yes, I am.*          *No, I'm not.*

2. **Should** I stay there?     _____     _____

3. **Can** I bring my medicines?     _____     _____

4. **Did** Patty visit you there?     _____     _____

5. **May** I ask you a question?     _____     _____

6. **Is** the question about Patty?     _____     _____

7. **Shouldn't** Patty answer that?     _____     _____

8. **Does** Patty want to answer?     _____     _____

9. **Couldn't** she come here?     _____     _____

10. **Do** you know her family?     _____     _____

11. **Are** you sure about that?     _____     _____

## H6. Noun adjectives. Insert the words in (...) inside the sentences.

1. I like the sweater. (**Paul**)     *I like Paul's sweater.*

2. You like the color. (**wall**)     _____

3. What's the number? (**page**)     _____

4. This is the picture. (**my uncle**)     _____

5. Look at the lamp. (**ceiling**)     _____

6. I drive the white car. (**girls**)     _____

7. We enjoy the class. (**Ms. Gray**)     _____

8. We love the class. (**art**)     _____

9. The noses are big. (**boys**)     _____

10. I like the furniture. (**bedroom**)     _____

11. We don't use cups. (**plastic**)     _____

12. I hate paper plates. (**Tom**)     _____

13. The parks are closed. (**city**)     _____

**H7.** Follow the example.

1.    Frank / sister / hurt

**stomach**

*Is Frank's sister sick?*
   Yes, she's sick.
*What is wrong with his sister?*
   Her stomach hurts.
*Shouldn't she see the doctor now?*
   In my opinion she should.

2.    boys / parents / hurt

**backs**

_____
_____
_____
_____
_____

3.    Paul  / aunt / hurt

**throat**

_____
_____
_____
_____
_____

4.    Cynthia / nephews / hurt

**bones**

_____
_____
_____
_____
_____

# Lesson #6

## Illnesses

## Index

## Audio & Translations

 **English Audio available online for sections A-E.**

 **Translations in various Languages available online for Sections A, B, and E.**

## www.BasicESL.com

**1.** flu

**2.** fever

**3.** chicken pox

**4.** mumps

**5.** bruise

**6.** stomach ache

**7.** headache

**8.** cold

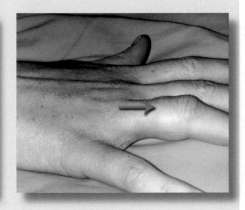

**9.** swelling

**10.** cut

**11.** fracture

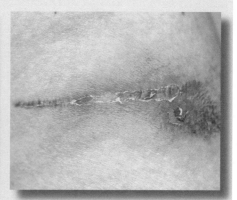

**12.** burn

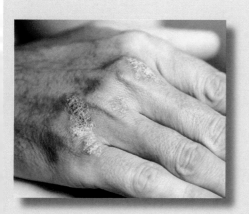

**13.** rash

**14.** asthma

**15.** deaf

**16.** lame

**17.** blind

**18.** hump-backed

## Vocabulary Study: Other Vocabulary

| | | | | | |
|---|---|---|---|---|---|
| 1. | n | chills | 11. | v | bleed |
| 2. | n | diarrhea | 12. | v | faint |
| 3. | n | headache | 13. | v | fast |
| 4. | n | indigestion | 14. | v | inject |
| 5. | n | tablet | 15. | v | know |
| 6. | n | wound | 16. | v | recover |
| 7. | adj | blind | 17. | v | risk |
| 8. | adj | deaf | 18. | v | sprain |
| 9. | adj | fortunate | 19. | v | twist |
| 10. | adj | lame | 20. | v | write (wrote) |

For the audio pronunciations and written translations of **Sections A and B,** please go to:

## www.basicesl.com

## Vocabulary Study: Other Vocabulary

| | | | | | |
|---|---|---|---|---|---|
| 1. | n | bandage | 11. | v | cure |
| 2. | n | cramps | 12. | v | deliver |
| 3. | n | cure | 13. | v | diagnose |
| 4. | n | cut | 14. | v | get better |
| 5. | n | digestion | 15. | v | get sick |
| 6. | n | ear ache | 16. | v | get worse |
| 7. | n | injury | 17. | v | heal |
| 8. | n | relief | 18. | v | injure |
| 9. | n | suffering | 19. | v | irritate |
| 10. | n | surgeon | 20. | v | suffer |

## B1. Modal Verb: "must" and "have to"

**i**

I **must** take this medicine.
I **have to** take this medicine.

You **must** go to the hospital.
You **have to** go to the hospital.

She **must** fast for 12 hours.
She **has to** fast for 12 hours.

John **must** have an operation.
John **has to** have an operation.

### B1 - B2

The modal verb **"must"** is used in the present tense to express **necessity** or **personal obligation** coming from the convictions of the speaker.

Its equivalent, **"have to,"** can be used in all tenses. It is more commonly used in the US. It expresses other obligations imposed by customs or laws.

## B2. "Must" and "have to": Questions

**i**

**Must** I take aspirin?
**Do I have to** take aspirin?

**Must she** lower the fever?
**Does she have to** lower the fever?

**Must** they cover their wounds?
**Do they have to** cover their wounds?

**Must** I take antibiotics?
**Do I have to** take antibiotics?

## B3. "Must": Negative Sentences

**i**

You **must not** ignore the pain.
You **mustn't** ignore the pain.

We **must** rest 8 hours a day.
We **mustn't** rest 5 hours a day.

Ann **must** stop walking.
She **mustn't** stop eating.

He **must** fight the infection.
He **mustn't** fight the low fever.

### B3

Negative sentences are formed with the word **"not"** after **"must."** The contraction of **"must not"** is **"mustn't."**

## B4. "Must": Long and Short Answers

**Must** I worry about the tumor?
  Yes, you **must** worry about the tumor.
  Yes, you **must**.

**Do** I **have** to see the doctor?
  Yes, you **have to** see the doctor.
  Yes, you **have to**.

**Must** Sara **pay** for the vaccine?
  Yes, she **must** pay for the vaccine.
  Yes, she **must**.

## B5. "Must": Long and Short Negative Answers

**Must** I stay in the hospital now?
  No, you **mustn't** stay in the hospital.
  No, you **mustn't**.

**Must** she clean the wound?
  No, she **must not** clean the wound.
  No, she **mustn't**.

**Do** I **have to** worry about the itching?
  No, you **don't have to** worry.
  No, you **don't have to**.

## B6. List of Irregular Verbs

Where **did** Henry **hide**?
  He **hid** under his bed.

Where **did** the woman **hold** the baby?
  She **held** the baby in her arms.

How much meat **did** they **grind**?
  They **ground** two pounds of meat.

**Did** America **fight** against England?
  Yes, it **fought** against England.

**B4 - B5**

*In questions, the sentence begins with the modal verb "must," followed by the subject and the main verb without "to."*

## C1. Read and Listen to the Story.

Alice is Mrs. Brown's small daughter. She is sick in bed. She twisted her ankle playing at school. When Mrs. Brown's children are sick, she takes her children to the doctor. When Alice arrived at the clinic, the doctor asked Alice, "What is wrong with you?" Alice replied, "I have a headache and my ankle hurts, too." "Do you feel any fever", the doctor asked again. Alice didn't know how to answer the question. Fortunately she didn't have any.

The doctor examined Alice's ankle. There was nothing serious with her ankle. The doctor advised her to rest at home. He also wrote a prescription for the headache. Alice must take two pills a day for the pain. Alice stayed in bed at home for two more days. She didn't go to school. When she recovered, Alice was very happy because she wanted to play again at school with her friends.

## C2. Read and Listen to the dialog.

**How does Alice feel?**
She does not feel well.

**What is wrong with her?**
She has a headache.

**Is that all?**
No, she twisted her ankle also.

**How did it happen?**
It happened at school.

**What did her mother do?**
She took her to the doctor.

**What was the doctor's advice?**
He advised Alice to rest in bed.

**How long should she stay in bed?**
She should stay in bed for two days.

**Should she take aspirin?**
She could take it, if needed.

**With food or without food?**
He recommended with food.

**Why was Alice happy?**
Because she recovered soon.

**D1.** Henry / bruise

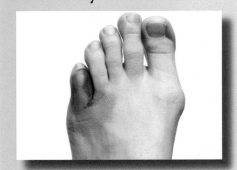

**Whose foot is this?**
   This is Henry's foot.

**What happened to his foot?**
   He bruised his foot.

**What should he do?**
   He must go to the doctor.
   He must not wait any longer.

**D2.** aunt / burn

**Whose hand is this?**
   This is my aunt's hand.

**What happened to her hand?**
   She burned her hand.

**What should she do?**
   She must go to the doctor.
   He must not wait any longer.

**D3.** boy / break

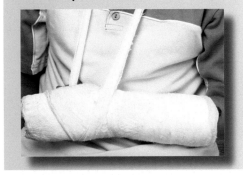

**Whose arm is this?**
   This is the boy's arm.

**What happened to his arm?**
   He broke his arm.

**What should he do?**
   He must go to the doctor.
   He mustn't wait any longer.

**D4.** brother / swell

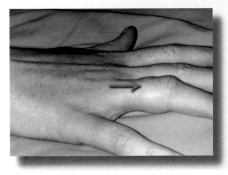

**Whose finger is this?**
   This is my brother's finger.

**What happened to his finger?**
   His finger swelled.

**What should he do?**
   He must go to the doctor.
   He mustn't wait any longer.

## Verb "to look"

1. What are you **looking for?**
2. **Look it up** in the dictionary.
3. I am going to **look into** this.
4. I am **looking forward** to my vacation.
5. My sister is **looking after** the baby.
6. He **looks down** on my brother.
7. **Look out** when you cross the street.

## Verb "to show"

1. Charles **showed up** late.
2. They like to **show off.**

**Phrasal verbs** or **prepositional verbs** are verbs followed by a preposition or an adverb. When the verb is followed by a preposition or adverb, the verb acquires a different meaning from the original meaning. When the object of the phrasal verb is a direct object pronoun, the pronoun is placed between the verb and the preposition.

For the English audio pronunciations and written native language translations of **section E,** please go to:

## www.basicesl.com

They like to **show off.**

I am going **to look into** this.

End of the **oral exercises** for lesson 6.
**You can find additional exercises in sections D, F & G at Basic ESL Online.**

Please continue with the **written exercises** for this lesson in **section H.**

## Lesson 6

## H1. Write the past tense of these irregular verbs.

| | | | | | |
|---|---|---|---|---|---|
| 1. | hide | _____ | drive | _____ |
| 2. | hold | _____ | drink | _____ |
| 3. | grind | _____ | draw | _____ |
| 4. | fight | _____ | eat | _____ |
| 5. | beat | _____ | fall | _____ |
| 6. | bite | _____ | hear | _____ |
| 7. | grow | _____ | feed | _____ |
| 8. | become | _____ | feel | _____ |

## H2. Change *must* for its equivalent.

1. You **must** take antibiotics.　　*You **have to** take*　antibiotics.
2. She **must** not rest in bed longer.　_____　in bed longer.
3. Mom **must** cover Ann's wound.　_____　Ann's wound.
4. Tony **must not** stop working.　_____　working.
5. I **must** go now to the hospital.　_____　now to the hospital.
6. Mom **must** talk to the doctor.　_____　to the doctor.
7. We **must** wait for his parents.　_____　for his parents.
8. We **must** not be impatient.　_____　impatient.

## H3. Make the sentence negative.

1. Mary **fought** fiercely.      *Mary **did not** fight fiercely.*
2. You **should** ignore the advice. _____
3. They **ought to** eat more. _____
4. I **can** walk far. _____
5. Henry **hid** under the bed. _____
6. She **drank** some water. _____
7. I **must** have an operation. _____
8. I **have** to take these pills. _____

## H4. Ask questions.

1. Mary **fought** fiercely.      ***Did** Mary **fight** fiercely?*
2. You **should** ignore the advice. _____
3. They **ought to** eat more. _____
4. I **can** walk far. _____
5. Henry **hid** under the bed. _____
6. She **drinks** some water. _____
7. I **must** have an operation. _____
8. I **have** to take these pills. _____

## H5. Express probability with the modal verb *must*.

1. *tired*    My sister works hard.      *She **must** be tired.*
2. *sad*    Tom is always crying. _____
3. *hungry*    The boys are always eating. _____
4. *slow*    John always comes late. _____
5. *smart*    Helen knows the answers. _____
6. *sick*    She has some fever. _____
7. *proud*    They passed a hard test _____

## H6. Indicate the location of these parts of the body.

| | Location | | Location | | Location |
|---|---|---|---|---|---|
| 1. wrist | **B** | chest | _____ | toe | _____ |
| 2. throat | _____ | ankle | _____ | bowels | _____ |
| 3. stomach | _____ | neck | _____ | feet | _____ |
| 4. hip | _____ | hair | _____ | finger | _____ |
| 5. kidney | _____ | shoulder | _____ | heart | _____ |
| 6. thigh | _____ | eye | _____ | knee | _____ |
| 7. back | _____ | hand | _____ | foot | _____ |

A

B

C

## H7. Select the best choice(s): *must, can, may, should, ought to,* or *have to.*

| | | | |
|---|---|---|---|
| 1. | invitation | You … come in now. | *may, can*_____ |
| 2. | obligation | You … behave well at school. | _____ |
| 3. | permission | When … I make a phone call? | _____ |
| 4. | advise | He … wait there longer. | _____ |
| 5. | permission | You … play there during that time. | _____ |
| 6. | necessity | Lynn has high fever. She … rest. | _____ |
| 7. | probability | She … not be there at that time. | _____ |
| 8. | advise | Where … I buy some good gloves? | _____ |
| 9. | advise | He … invite my friends to the party. | _____ |
| 10. | strong obligation | Mary … not work if she is sick. | _____ |

## H8. Answer the following questions.

Alice is Mrs. Brown's small daughter. She is hurt in bed. She twisted her ankle playing at school. When Mrs. Brown's children are hurt, she takes them to the doctor. The doctor examined Alice's ankle.

The doctor advised her to rest at home. Alice stayed in bed for six days. When she recovered, Alice was very happy because she could play at school with her friends.

1. *Who is Alice?*

_____

2. *Where is Alice?*

_____

3. *What happened to Alice?*

_____

4. *What did the doctor do at the clinic?*

_____

5. *What was the doctor's advice to Alice?*

_____

6. *How long did she stay resting at home?*

_____

_____

## H9. Answer the following questions.

1. How much does the _____ medicine cost?      child, children's, childrens'

2. The _____ throat is infected and it hurts.      man's, Nancy's, boys'

3. __ arm is broken. She should go to the hospital.      Paul's, Nancy's, Boy's

4. Why don't we call the _____ doctor first?      Mary, Nancy's, family

5. ___ leg was swollen yesterday. It's getting better.      Student's, Girl's, Lynn's

6. She is sick. She _____ work today.      must, shouldn't, ought

7. You ____ to study more if you don't want to fail.      must, should, have

8. He _ to rest longer in bed if he wants to recover.      must, have, ought

9. _____ I ask you a question about your plans?      Ought, Can, Might

10. My brother cannot come. He ___ be very busy.      should, ought, must

# Chapter 3
# The Time

Lesson 7:    Time of Day
Lesson 8:    The Week
Lesson 9:    The Months of the year

# What to do in each section of every lesson...

## A - Vocabulary Study

Section A includes the vocabulary that will be used throughout the lesson. Learning new vocabulary is basic to learning a new language.

**Read** the vocabulary several times.
If you are on Basic ESL Online:
**Listen** to the **English audio pronunciation**.
**View** the **native language translations** of the vocabulary.

Listen and read the vocabulary until you can understand the vocabulary without looking at the words.

## B - Sentence Structure

Section B teaches students basic English sentences using the vocabulary in section A.

**Read** and **study** the sentences.
If you are on Basic ESL Online:
**Listen** to the **English audio pronunciation**.
**View** the **native language translations** of the sentences.
**View** the **grammar concepts** by clicking on the **information button**  .

Repeat the sentences as many times as needed.
Continue to the next section once you can **understand** the sentences without looking at them.

## C - Listening Exercises

**Read** the story or dialog several times.
If you are on Basic ESL Online, **listen** to the story or dialog while reading it several times.

Once you are familiar with the story or dialog, try to see if you can **understand** it by only listening without reading.

## D - Conversation Exercises

**Read** the conversation dialogs several times.
If you are on Basic ESL Online, **listen** to the dialogs until you can understand them without looking at them.

Finally, try to **speak** the conversation dialogs by only looking at the pictures and key words.

## E - Common Phrases

Many of the **common phrases** that are presented in this section are frequently used by the native English speakers in their everyday life.

**Read** the common phrases several times.
If you are on Basic ESL Online, **listen** to the common phrases while reading. **Listen** as many times as needed until you can understand the common phrases without looking at the sentences.

## H - Written Exercises

The written exercises provide an opportunity to test what you learned in the lesson. You can never be sure of knowing something unless you can put it in writing.

You can check your answers by going to the **Answer Key Section** in the back of the workbook.

For information regarding **Basic ESL Online,** please visit **www.basicesl.com**.
Audio Pronunciaton of English & Native Language Translations.

# Lesson #7

# Time of The Day

## Index

## Audio & Translations

 English Audio available online for sections A-E.

 Translations in various Languages available online for Sections A, B, and E.

### www.BasicESL.com

**1.** two o'clock

**2.** five past two

**3.** ten past two

**4.** a quarter past two

**5.** twenty past two

**6.** twenty-five past two

**7.** half past two

**8.** twenty five to three

**9.** twenty to three

**10.** a quarter to three

**11.** ten to three

**12.** five to three

**13.** in the morning

**14.** at noon

**15.** in the evening

**16.** in the afternoon

**17.** at midnight

**18.** at night

## Vocabulary Study: Other Vocabulary

| | | | | | |
|---|---|---|---|---|---|
| 1. | n | alarm clock | 11. | v | end |
| 2. | n | break | 12. | v | get up (got) |
| 3. | n | half an hour | 13. | v | return |
| 4. | n | hour | 14. | v | shout |
| 5. | n | late | 15. | v | sleep (slept) |
| 6. | n | minute | 16. | v | solve |
| 7. | n | problem | 17. | v | wake up (woke) |
| 8. | n | second | 18. | adv | early |
| 9. | v | be slow | 19. | adv | sometimes |
| 10. | n | dream | 20. | con | however |

For the audio pronunciations and written translations of **Sections A and B,** please go to:

# www.basicesl.com

## Vocabulary Study: Other Vocabulary

| | | | | | |
|---|---|---|---|---|---|
| 1. | n | deceit | 11. | v | afford |
| 2. | adj | cumbersome | 12. | v | apply |
| 3. | adj | interested | 13. | v | attend |
| 4. | adj | obedient | 14. | v | deceive |
| 5. | adj | safe | 15. | v | embarrass |
| 6. | adj | shy | 16. | v | obey |
| 7. | adj | simple | 17. | v | remove |
| 8. | adj | skinny | 18. | v | tend |
| 9. | adj | sparse | 19. | v | train |
| 10. | adj | uptight | 20. | adv | gently |

## B1. Telling Time: **Time of the Day**

**i**

| am | in the **morning** |
| pm | in the **afternoon** |
| pm | in the **evening** |
| pm | at **night** |

| 1:00 am | It is one o'clock in the **morning.** |
| 1:00 pm | It is one o'clock in the **afternoon.** |
| 6:00 pm | It is six o'clock in the **evening.** |
| 9:00 pm | It is nine o'clock at **night.** |

**B1**

*The time of the day is divided into four parts:*
**Morning**
*(from 12:00 am to 12:00 noon)*
**Afternoon**
*(from noon to 5:00)*
**Evening**
*(from 5:00 pm to dark)*
**Night**
*(from dark to midnight)*

## B2. Telling Time: **Present Tense**

**i**

What time **does** Ann **get up**?
   She **gets up** at 7:00.

What time **does** she **have** breakfast?
   She **has** breakfast at 8:00.

What time **does** she **go** to work?
   She **goes** to work at 9:00

What time **does** she **eat** lunch?
   She **eats** lunch at noon.

**B2 - B3**

*When we want to inquire about the time of day, or what time the action of the verb takes place, we use these expressions:*

**1. Time of day:**
  *"What time is it?"*

**2. Time of the action:**
  *"(At) What time do you eat?"*

## B3. Telling Time: **Present Tense**

**i**

What time **does** she **leave** the office?
   She **leaves** the office at 6:00.

What time **does** she **arrive** home?
   She **arrives** home at 8:00.

What time **does** she **eat** dinner?
   She **eats** dinner at 9:00.

What time **does** she **go** to bed?
   She **goes** to bed at midnight.

## B4. Telling Time: **Past Tense**

What time **did** you **get up** yesterday?
I **got up** at 9:00 am.

What time **did** you **have** breakfast?
I **had** breakfast at 8:30.

What time **did** you **leave** for work?
I **left** for work at 10:15.

What time **did** you **eat** lunch?
I **ate** lunch at noon.

## B5. List of Irregular Verbs

**Did** she **keep** the promise?
Yes, she **kept** the promise.

At what time **did** you **leave** the office?
I **left** the office at noon.

What **did** Ann **lose**?
She **lost** her car keys.

**Did** they **make** a mistake?
Yes, they **made** a mistake.

For the pronunciation and
translation of
**the sections A and B,**
please go to:

# www.basicesl.com

## B6. List of Irregular Verbs

How long **did** you **kneel**?
I **knelt** for two hours.

**Did** you **lead** the boy's group?
No, my brother **led** the group.

**Did** you **lend** money to Greg?
Yes, I **lent** some money to Greg.

**Did** you **light** the candles yesterday?
Yes, I **lit** the candles yesterday.

## C1. Read and Listen to the story.

My two brothers Mike and Tom are still sleeping at 7:00 am. The alarm clock wakes up my brothers twenty minutes later. Sometimes they arrive at school late because the clock is ten minutes slow. Their first class starts at 8:30.

The school bell rings at 9:15 for a ten minute break. At 9:25 they return to the math class. They do lots of math problems. My brothers are smart. They solve all the problems in half an hour.

There are no classes at noon time. The students go to the cafeteria for lunch. After lunch they have three quarters of an hour to play on the playground. The last class ends at 2:45 pm. They return home at 3:15 pm. When they arrive home from school their mom is waiting for them at the door.

## C2. Read and Listen to the dialog.

**How many brothers do you have?**
I have two brothers.

**What are their names?**
Their names are Tony and Mike.

**What time do they wake up?**
They wake up at 7:20.

**Do they arrive at school on time?**
No, sometimes they are late.

**Why are they late?**
Because their alarm clock is slow.

**When does the first class start?**
It starts at 8:30 am.

**How long does it last?**
It lasts fifty-five minutes.

**What do they do afterwards?**
They have a fifteen minute break.

**Which is the next class?**
It is the math class.

**What time does the school end?**
The school ends at 2:45 pm.

**D1.** you / get up (7:00)

***What time is it in the first picture?***
It is six fifteen in the morning.

***What time do you usually get up?***
I usually get up at seven o'clock.

***What time did you get up yesterday?***
I got up at the same time.

**D2.** Alex / lunch (12:00)

***What time is it in the second picture?***
It is nine thirty in the morning.

***What time does Alex usually eat lunch?***
He usually eats lunch at twelve o'clock.

***What time did he eat lunch yesterday?***
He ate lunch at the same time.

**D3.** boys / play (2:45)

***What time is it in the third picture?***
It is three o'clock in the afternoon.

***What time do the boys usually play?***
They usually play at a quarter to three.

***What time did they play yesterday?***
They played at the same time.

**D4.** Carol / bed (9:00)

***What time is it in the fourth picture?***
It is ten minutes to nine in the evening.

***What time does Carol usually go to bed?***
She usually goes to bed at nine o'clock.

***What time did she go to bed yesterday?***
She went to bed at the same time.

## Verb "to put"

1. Please, **put out** the cigarette.
2. I cannot **put down** the book.
3. You have to **put up with** the boss.
4. **Put up** the ladder please.
5. Every week they **put aside** 20 dollars.
6. His dirty jokes **put** me **off**.
7. My dad is **putting off** his trip.
8. He is **putting together** a competition.
9. She **puts on** weight easily.

**Phrasal verbs** or **prepositional verbs** are verbs followed by a preposition or an adverb. When the verb is followed by a preposition or adverb, the verb acquires a different meaning from the original meaning. When the object of the phrasal verb is a direct object pronoun, the pronoun is placed between the verb and the preposition.

For the English audio pronunciations and written native language translations of **section E,** please go to:

## www.basicesl.com

Please, **put out** the cigarette.

End of the **oral exercises** for lesson 7.
**You can find additional exercises in sections D, F & G at Basic ESL Online.**

Please continue with the **written exercises** for this lesson in **section H.**

Lesson

**7**

## H1. Write the past tense of these irregular verbs.

1. keep _____     get _____
2. leave _____     fall _____
3. lose _____     hear _____
4. make _____     feel _____
5. kneel _____     hide _____
6. lead _____     hold _____
7. lend _____     grind _____
8. light _____     fight _____

## H2. Answer the questions.

1. How many **hours** are there in a day?

    *There are **twenty-four** hours in a day.*

2. How many **minutes** are there in one hour?

    _____

3. How many **minutes** are there in a **quarter** of an hour?

    _____

4. How many **seconds** are there in one minute?

    _____

## H3. *What time is it?* Answer the question with the words in (...).

1. (2:00 a.m.)  *It is two o'clock in the morning.*

2. (12:00 p.m.)  _____

3. (1:30 p.m.)  _____

4. (6:15 p.m.)  _____

5. (9:45 p.m.)  _____

6. (12:00 a.m.)  _____

## H4. Complete with prepositions.

|  | in | far |
|---|---|---|
| 1. Lisa works … a factory … away. | ____ | ____ |
| 2. Today she has a day … from work … the factory. | ____ | ____ |
| 3. She lives … her parents … a big house. | ____ | ____ |
| 4. She gets … early …. the morning. | ____ | ____ |
| 5. She takes her daughter … school … car. | ____ | ____ |
| 6. Lisa calls her mom … the phone …nine thirty. | ____ | ____ |
| 7. Lisa asks her mom … her plans … today. | ____ | ____ |
| 8. Today she wants to take her mom … a restaurant … dinner. | ____ | ____ |
| 9. It is close … her home and far … the factory. | ____ | ____ |
| 10. Lisa is very popular … that restaurant … the clients. | ____ | ____ |
| 11. She leaves home … 12:00 noon to be there … time. | ____ | ____ |
| 12. She doesn't return home … 4:00 p.m. … the afternoon. | ____ | ____ |
| 13. She sits … the sofa and reads … an hour. | ____ | ____ |

**H5.** *Ann's daily schedule.* Follow the example.

**1.**      6:15 / get up

**7:00 am**

*What time is it now?*
   *It is* **six fifteen** *in the morning.*

*At what time does* **Ann** *get up?*
   *She* **gets up** *at seven o'clock in the morning.*

**2.**      9:30 / eat breakfast

**8:15 am**

_____

_____

_____

_____

**3.**      12:00 / have lunch

**12:30 pm**

_____

_____

_____

_____

**4.**      5:10 / study

**5:45 pm**

_____

_____

_____

_____

**5.**      8:20 / go to bed

**9:00 pm**

_____

_____

_____

_____

## H6. Change "*every day*" for "*yesterday*".

**Every day** my two brothers Mike and Tom are still sleeping at 7:00 am when they hear the alarm clock. Once in a while, they arrive at school late because the clock is ten minutes slow. Their first class begins at 8:30.

The school bell rings at 9:15 for a ten minute break. At 9:25 they come back to the math class. They do lots of math problems. They solve all the problems in half an hour.

The students go to the cafeteria for lunch at noon time. After lunch they have three quarters of an hour to play on the playground.

The last class ends at 2:45 pm. They leave school for home at 3:15.

*Yesterday* _____

_____

_____

_____

_____

_____

_____

_____

_____

_____

_____

_____

_____

_____

_____

_____

_____

_____

_____

_____

# Lesson #8

## The Week

## Index

## Audio & Translations

 **English Audio available online for sections A-E.**

 **Translations in various Languages available online for Sections A, B, and E.**

## www.BasicESL.com

**1.** the week

**2.** the weekend

**3.** Sunday

**4.** Monday

**5.** Tuesday

**6.** Wednesday

**7.** Thursday

**8.** Friday

**9.** Saturday

| FEBRUARY | | | | | | |
|---|---|---|---|---|---|---|
| Sun | Mon | Tue | Wed | Thu | Fri | Sat |
| | | | | | 1 | 2 |
| 3 | 4 | 5 | 6 | 7 | 8 | 9 |
| 10 | 11 | ⑫ | 13 | 14 | 15 | 16 |
| 17 | 18 | 19 | 20 | 21 | 22 | 23 |
| 24 | 25 | 26 | 27 | 28 | | |

**10.** today

| FEBRUARY | | | | | | |
|---|---|---|---|---|---|---|
| Sun | Mon | Tue | Wed | Thu | Fri | Sat |
| | | | | | 1 | 2 |
| 3 | 4 | 5 | 6 | 7 | 8 | 9 |
| 10 | 11 | 12 | ⑬ | 14 | 15 | 16 |
| 17 | 18 | 19 | 20 | 21 | 22 | 23 |
| 24 | 25 | 26 | 27 | 28 | | |

**11.** tomorrow

| FEBRUARY | | | | | | |
|---|---|---|---|---|---|---|
| Sun | Mon | Tue | Wed | Thu | Fri | Sat |
| | | | | | 1 | 2 |
| 3 | 4 | 5 | 6 | 7 | 8 | 9 |
| 10 | 11 | 12 | 13 | ⑭ | 15 | 16 |
| 17 | 18 | 19 | 20 | 21 | 22 | 23 |
| 24 | 25 | 26 | 27 | 28 | | |

**12.** after tomorrow (*the day*)

| FEBRUARY | | | | | | |
|---|---|---|---|---|---|---|
| Sun | Mon | Tue | Wed | Thu | Fri | Sat |
| | | | | | 1 | 2 |
| 3 | 4 | 5 | 6 | 7 | 8 | 9 |
| 10 | ⑪ | 12 | 13 | 14 | 15 | 16 |
| 17 | 18 | 19 | 20 | 21 | 22 | 23 |
| 24 | 25 | 26 | 27 | 28 | | |

**13.** yesterday

| FEBRUARY | | | | | | |
|---|---|---|---|---|---|---|
| Sun | Mon | Tue | Wed | Thu | Fri | Sat |
| | | | | | 1 | 2 |
| 3 | 4 | 5 | 6 | 7 | 8 | 9 |
| ⑩ | 11 | 12 | 13 | 14 | 15 | 16 |
| 17 | 18 | 19 | 20 | 21 | 22 | 23 |
| 24 | 25 | 26 | 27 | 28 | | |

**14.** before yesterday (*the day*)

| FEBRUARY | | | | | | |
|---|---|---|---|---|---|---|
| Sun | Mon | Tue | Wed | Thu | Fri | Sat |
| | | | | | 1 | 2 |
| 3 | 4 | 5 | 6 | 7 | 8 | 9 |
| 10 | 11 | ⑫ | 13 | 14 | 15 | 16 |
| → 17 | 18 | 19 | 20 | 21 | 22 | 23 ← |
| 24 | 25 | 26 | 27 | 28 | | |

**15.** next week

**16.** now (*2:00 pm*)

**17.** soon (*2:25 pm*)

**18.** later (*5:10 pm*)

## Vocabulary Study: Other Vocabulary

| | | | | | | |
|---|---|---|---|---|---|
| 1. | n | anesthesia | 11. | adj | numbed |
| 2. | n | appointment | 12. | v | avoid |
| 3. | n | assistant | 13. | v | break (broke) |
| 4. | n | cavity | 14. | v | find (found) |
| 5. | n | dentist | 15. | v | hate |
| 6. | n | future | 16. | v | identify |
| 7. | n | gum | 17. | v | numb |
| 8. | n | molar | 18. | v | protect |
| 9. | n | piece | 19. | v | recommend |
| 10. | adj | broken | 20. | | as a rule |

For the audio pronunciations and written translations of **Sections A and B,** please go to:

## www.basicesl.com

## Vocabulary Study: Other Vocabulary

| | | | | | | |
|---|---|---|---|---|---|
| 1. | n | joke | 11. | v | aim |
| 2. | n | meeting | 12. | v | comfort |
| 3. | n | mind | 13. | v | give (gave) |
| 4. | n | shot | 14. | v | hug |
| 5. | n | whip | 15. | v | lick |
| 6. | adj | biased | 16. | v | mind |
| 7. | adj | grumpy | 17. | v | reduce |
| 8. | adj | naughty | 18. | v | whisper |
| 9. | adj | skinny | 19. | adv | gently |
| 10. | adj | vengeful | 20. | | in order to |

## B1. Subject and Object Pronoun Forms

| Subject | Object |
|---------|--------|
| I | me |
| you | you |
| he | him |
| she | her |
| it | it |
| we | us |
| you | you |
| they | them |

**B1 - B2 - B3**

*Object pronouns* replace nouns that are the object of the verb. They always go after the verb or after a preposition.

## B2. Object Nouns (ON) and Object Pronouns (OP)

| | |
|---|---|
| ON | I know **your nephew.** |
| OP | I know **him.** |
| ON | I know **Mary.** |
| OP | I know **her.** |
| ON | I know **the lesson.** |
| OP | I know **it.** |
| ON | I know **the boys.** |
| OP | I know **them.** |

## B3. Object Nouns (N) and Object Pronouns (P)

| | |
|---|---|
| ON | She knows **Tom and me.** |
| OP | She knows **us.** |
| ON | She knows **Greg and you.** |
| OP | She knows **you.** |
| ON | She knows **Paul and Ann.** |
| OP | She knows **them.** |
| ON | She knows **the nephews.** |
| OP | She knows **them.** |

## B4. Irregular Verbs: Answer with Object Pronouns

Did the owner **pay** the **workers**?
Yes, he **paid them** on Sunday.

Where did Carol **meet Paul**?
She **met him** at church.

When did Fred **quit** the **job**?
He **quit it** last month.

Where did mom **put** the **letters**?
She **put them** in a box.

## B5. Object Pronouns with Phrasal Verbs

Did you wake up **John**?
Yes, I woke **him** up.

Did you tear up the **letters**?
Yes, I tore **them** up.

Did he put out the **cigar**?
Yes, he put **it** out.

Did she give back the **coins**?
Yes, she gave **them** back.

### B5

*Phrasal verbs or prepositional verbs are those followed by a preposition or an adverb. When they are together, the verb acquires a different meaning than the original main verb. When the object of the phrasal verb is a direct object pronoun, the pronoun is placed between the verb and the preposition.*

## B6. List of Irregular Verbs

How many books **did** you **read**?
I **read** five books, at least.

**Did** you **ring** the bell last night?
Yes, I **rang** the bell last night.

At what time **did** the sun **rise**?
It **rose** at 5:30 am.

**Did** he **mean** that?
Yes, he **meant** that.

## C1. Read and Listen to the story.

Today is Saturday, the last day of the week. My name is Carol. As a rule I hate to go to the dentist, but last Tuesday I didn't have any choice. While I was having lunch at work, one of my upper molars broke into two pieces. It hurt very badly. I couldn't eat any more. It was painful. I immediately stopped eating and went home. I called the dentist and made an appointment for Wednesday. When I arrived at the office, the dentist's assistant took X-rays of my teeth.  A few minutes later, the dentist examined them.  Besides the broken molar, he found two other molars with cavities.

He gave me a shot of anesthesia. I didn't feel any pain while he worked on my teeth. The left side of my mouth was completely numbed. Before leaving the office, the dentist advised me to avoid eating hard foods for the next two days, Thursday and Friday. He also prescribed some pills for pain if I needed them. He also recommended cleaning my teeth daily in order to protect the gums and avoid more cavities in the future.

## C2. Read and Listen to the dialog.

*Does Carol hate the dentist?*
No, she doesn't. She likes him.

*What does she hate then?*
She hates going to the dentist.

*When did she go to the dentist?*
She went last Tuesday.

*Why did she go?*
She broke one of her molars.

*How did she do it?*
She bit bone at lunch.

*Did it hurt?*
Yes, it hurt a lot.

*Did she call the dentist?*
Yes, she did. It was hurting badly.

*Did she get an appointment?*
Yes, she got it for the next day.

*What day was it?*
It was last Wednesday.

*What did the dentist do?*
He extracted the broken molar.

*What did the dentist find?*
He found some cavities also.

*Did he prescribe any pills?*
He prescribed pills for pain.

**D1.** 2/8 - see (parents) - 2/6

FEBRUARY

| Sun | Mon | Tue | Wed | Thu | Fri | Sat |
|-----|-----|-----|-----|-----|-----|-----|
|     |     |     |     |     | 1   | 2   |
| 3   | 4   | 5   | 6   | 7   | (8) | 9   |
| 10  | 11  | 12  | 13  | 14  | 15  | 16  |
| 17  | 18  | 19  | 20  | 21  | 22  | 23  |
| 24  | 25  | 26  | 27  | 28  |     |     |

**What day is today?**
It's the 8th of February.

**What day of the week is it?**
It is Friday.

**When did you see your parents?**
I saw them the day before yesterday.

**D2.** 2/20 - speak (Carol) - 2/19

FEBRUARY

| Sun | Mon | Tue | Wed | Thu | Fri | Sat |
|-----|-----|-----|-----|-----|-----|-----|
|     |     |     |     |     | 1   | 2   |
| 3   | 4   | 5   | 6   | 7   | 8   | 9   |
| 10  | 11  | 12  | 13  | 14  | 15  | 16  |
| 17  | 18  | 19  | (20)| 21  | 22  | 23  |
| 24  | 25  | 26  | 27  | 28  |     |     |

**What day is today?**
It's the 20th of February.

**What day of the week is it?**
It is Wednesday.

**When did you speak to Carol?**
I spoke to her yesterday.

**D3.** 2/12 - visit (brother) - 2/13

FEBRUARY

| Sun | Mon | Tue | Wed | Thu | Fri | Sat |
|-----|-----|-----|-----|-----|-----|-----|
|     |     |     |     |     | 1   | 2   |
| 3   | 4   | 5   | 6   | 7   | 8   | 9   |
| 10  | 11  | (12)| 13  | 14  | 15  | 16  |
| 17  | 18  | 19  | 20  | 21  | 22  | 23  |
| 24  | 25  | 26  | 27  | 28  |     |     |

**What day is today?**
It's the 12th of February.

**What day of the week is it?**
It's Tuesday.

**When are you going to visit your brother?**
I am going to visit him tomorrow.

**D4.** 2/25 - prepare (lesson) - 2/27

FEBRUARY

| Sun | Mon | Tue | Wed | Thu | Fri | Sat |
|-----|-----|-----|-----|-----|-----|-----|
|     |     |     |     |     | 1   | 2   |
| 3   | 4   | 5   | 6   | 7   | 8   | 9   |
| 10  | 11  | 12  | 13  | 14  | 15  | 16  |
| 17  | 18  | 19  | 20  | 21  | 22  | 23  |
| 24  | (25)| 26  | 27  | 28  |     |     |

**What day is today?**
It's the 25th of February.

**What day of the week is it?**
It is Monday.

**When are you going to prepare the lesson?**
I am going to prepare it the day after tomorrow.

## Verb "to take"

1. The plane **took off** at 2:00 pm.
2. The boy **took apart** the toy.
3. I have to **take back** the book.
4. We **took out** 50 dollars from the bank.
5. Germany **took over** Poland in 1939.
6. This table **takes up** a lot of space.

## Verb "to tear"

1. The city **tore down** the theater.
2. The crocodile **tore off** my leg.
3. Did you **tear up** all the records?

**Phrasal verbs** or **prepositional verbs** are verbs followed by a preposition or an adverb. When the verb is followed by a preposition or adverb, the verb acquires a different meaning from the original meaning. When the object of the phrasal verb is a direct object pronoun, the pronoun is placed between the verb and the preposition.

For the English audio pronunciations and written native language translations of **section E,** please go to:

## www.basicesl.com

The plane **took off** at 2:00 pm.

We **took out** 50 dollars from the bank.

End of the **oral exercises** for lesson 8.
**You can find additional exercises in sections D, F & G at Basic ESL Online.**

Please continue with the **written exercises** for this lesson in **section H.**

**Lesson 8**

## H1. Write the past tense of these irregular verbs.

| | | | | |
|---|---|---|---|---|
| 1. | pay | _____ | keep | _____ |
| 2. | meet | _____ | leave | _____ |
| 3. | quit | _____ | lose | _____ |
| 4. | put | _____ | make | _____ |
| 5. | read | _____ | kneel | _____ |
| 6. | ring | _____ | lead | _____ |
| 7. | rise | _____ | lend | _____ |
| 8. | mean | _____ | light | _____ |

## H2. Replace the *object noun* with the *object pronoun*.

1. I know **Mary.**     *I know **her.***
2. I know **John.**     _____
3. I know **the school.**     _____
4. I know **your son.**     _____
5. I know **your daughter.**     _____
6. I know **Mary and John.**     _____
7. I know **the two cities.**     _____
8. I know **your children.**     _____

## H3. Replace the *object noun* with the *object pronoun.*

1. My brother wears **the black suit**.     *My brother wears it.*
2. Tony lives with **her sister**. _____
3. Her uncle knows **Joe and me**. _____
4. Don't open **the book** yet. _____
5. I saw **Henry** last week. _____
6. I also met **your niece Carol**. _____
7. She was with **her friends**. _____
8. She answered **all my questions**. _____
9. She is living with **her aunt**. _____
10. I paid **all my debts**. _____
11. We met **John's niece**. _____
12. Please, don't ring **the bell**. _____

## H4. Replace all subject nouns and object nouns with *pronouns.*

1. **Paul** fears the **chest pains**.     *He fears them.*
2. **Helen** loves **her house**. _____
3. **That man** lost **his arm**. _____
4. **The men** quit **their jobs**. _____
5. **The city** canceled **the parades**. _____
6. **My dad** punished **Joe and Tom**. _____
7. **Tom** was upset with **my dad**. _____
8. **They boys** are working for **John**. _____
9. **Sara's son** bought the **flowers**. _____
10. **George** likes **the white shoes**. _____
11. **The boys** don't bother **me and Ann**. _____

## H5. Complete with object pronouns.

1. **Your cousins** are here. Play with …        *them.*

2. **I** am an expert. Ask …                     _____

3. This is **your homework**. Finish …           _____

4. **Mary** is in France. Write to …             _____

5. **All the windows** are closed. Please, open …  _____

6. **Gregory** is sick. Why don't you visit …    _____

7. **This car** doesn't work. Can you fix …      _____

## H6. Make correct sentences.

1. it-he-much-likes-very            _____

2. now-them-wants-she               _____

3. Bob's-belong-to-they-uncle       _____

4. with-he-eats-us                  _____

5. him-not-need-you-do              _____

6. church-met-Tony's-I -sister-in   _____

7. day-is-what-today?               _____

## H7. Replace the object noun with the object pronoun.

1. Look up **the word** in the book.   *Look **it** up in the book.*

2. The lion tore off **his legs**.     _____

3. The city tears down **the buildings**.  _____

4. He threw up **the food**.           _____

5. Don't give up **your rights**.      _____

6. Please, put out **the candles**.    _____

7. Why don't you help out **Jane**?    _____

## H8. Follow the example.

1. Steve / put off / trip

**Sunday**

*Did Steve **put off** the **trip**?*
*Yes, he **put if off**.*

*When did he **put off** the **trip**?*
*He put **it** off on Sunday.*

2. you / cross out / mistake

**Monday**

3. mom / wake up / daughter

**Tuesday**

4. Anne / tear up / letters

**last weekend**

5. Greg / give away / car

**yesterday**

# Lesson #9

## Months

June

Mo Tu We Th Fr Sa Su

1  2
3  4  5  6  7  8  9
10 11 12 13 14 15 16
17 18 19 20 21 22 23
24 25 26 27 28 29 30

## Index

## Audio & Translations

English Audio available online for sections A-E.

Translations in various Languages available online for Sections A, B, and E.

**www.BasicESL.com**

**JANUARY**

| Sun | Mon | Tue | Wed | Thu | Fri | Sat |
|-----|-----|-----|-----|-----|-----|-----|
|  |  | 1 | 2 | 3 | 4 | 5 |
| 6 | 7 | 8 | 9 | 10 | 11 | 12 |
| 13 | 14 | 15 | 16 | 17 | 18 | 19 |
| 20 | 21 | 22 | 23 | 24 | 25 | 26 |
| 27 | 28 | 29 | 30 | 31 |  |  |

**1.** January

**FEBRUARY**

| Sun | Mon | Tue | Wed | Thu | Fri | Sat |
|-----|-----|-----|-----|-----|-----|-----|
|  |  |  |  |  | 1 | 2 |
| 3 | 4 | 5 | 6 | 7 | 8 | 9 |
| 10 | 11 | 12 | 13 | 14 | 15 | 16 |
| 17 | 18 | 19 | 20 | 21 | 22 | 23 |
| 24 | 25 | 26 | 27 | 28 |  |  |

**2.** February

**MARCH**

| Sun | Mon | Tue | Wed | Thu | Fri | Sat |
|-----|-----|-----|-----|-----|-----|-----|
|  |  |  |  |  | 1 | 2 |
| 3 | 4 | 5 | 6 | 7 | 8 | 9 |
| 10 | 11 | 12 | 13 | 14 | 15 | 16 |
| 17 | 18 | 19 | 20 | 21 | 22 | 23 |
| 24 | 25 | 26 | 27 | 28 | 29 | 30 |
| 31 |  |  |  |  |  |  |

**3.** March

**APRIL**

| Sun | Mon | Tue | Wed | Thu | Fri | Sat |
|-----|-----|-----|-----|-----|-----|-----|
|  | 1 | 2 | 3 | 4 | 5 | 6 |
| 7 | 8 | 9 | 10 | 11 | 12 | 13 |
| 14 | 15 | 16 | 17 | 18 | 19 | 20 |
| 21 | 22 | 23 | 24 | 25 | 26 | 27 |
| 28 | 29 | 30 |  |  |  |  |

**4.** April

**MAY**

| Sun | Mon | Tue | Wed | Thu | Fri | Sat |
|-----|-----|-----|-----|-----|-----|-----|
|  |  |  | 1 | 2 | 3 | 4 |
| 5 | 6 | 7 | 8 | 9 | 10 | 11 |
| 12 | 13 | 14 | 15 | 16 | 17 | 18 |
| 19 | 20 | 21 | 22 | 23 | 24 | 25 |
| 26 | 27 | 28 | 29 | 30 | 31 |  |

**5.** May

**JUNE**

| Sun | Mon | Tue | Wed | Thu | Fri | Sat |
|-----|-----|-----|-----|-----|-----|-----|
|  |  |  |  |  |  | 1 |
| 2 | 3 | 4 | 5 | 6 | 7 | 8 |
| 9 | 10 | 11 | 12 | 13 | 14 | 15 |
| 16 | 17 | 18 | 19 | 20 | 21 | 22 |
| 23 | 24 | 25 | 26 | 27 | 28 | 29 |
| 30 |  |  |  |  |  |  |

**6.** June

**JULY**

| Sun | Mon | Tue | Wed | Thu | Fri | Sat |
|-----|-----|-----|-----|-----|-----|-----|
|  | 1 | 2 | 3 | 4 | 5 | 6 |
| 7 | 8 | 9 | 10 | 11 | 12 | 13 |
| 14 | 15 | 16 | 17 | 18 | 19 | 20 |
| 21 | 22 | 23 | 24 | 25 | 26 | 27 |
| 28 | 29 | 30 | 31 |  |  |  |

**7.** July

**AUGUST**

| Sun | Mon | Tue | Wed | Thu | Fri | Sat |
|-----|-----|-----|-----|-----|-----|-----|
|  |  |  |  | 1 | 2 | 3 |
| 4 | 5 | 6 | 7 | 8 | 9 | 10 |
| 11 | 12 | 13 | 14 | 15 | 16 | 17 |
| 18 | 19 | 20 | 21 | 22 | 23 | 24 |
| 25 | 26 | 27 | 28 | 29 | 30 | 31 |

**8.** August

**SEPTEMBER**

| Sun | Mon | Tue | Wed | Thu | Fri | Sat |
|-----|-----|-----|-----|-----|-----|-----|
| 1 | 2 | 3 | 4 | 5 | 6 | 7 |
| 8 | 9 | 10 | 11 | 12 | 13 | 14 |
| 15 | 16 | 17 | 18 | 19 | 20 | 21 |
| 22 | 23 | 24 | 25 | 26 | 27 | 28 |
| 29 | 30 |  |  |  |  |  |

**9.** September

**10.** October

**11.** November

**12.** December

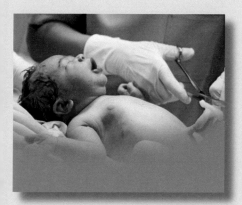

**13.** birth

**14.** kindergarten

**15.** college

**16.** graduation

**17.** to get married

**18.** to find a job

## Vocabulary Study: Other Vocabulary

| 1. | n | army | 11. | adj | wealthy |
|----|---|------|-----|-----|---------|
| 2. | n | funeral | 12. | v | be born |
| 3. | n | general | 13. | v | become |
| 4. | n | independence | 14. | v | bury |
| 5. | n | journey | 15. | v | consider |
| 6. | n | revolution | 16. | v | die |
| 7. | n | soldier | 17. | v | fall (fell) |
| 8. | n | tobacco | 18. | v | marry |
| 9. | n | war | 19. | v | remain |
| 10. | n | widow | 20. | v | take place |

For the audio pronunciations and written translations of **Sections A and B,** please go to:

## www.basicesl.com

## Vocabulary Study: Other Vocabulary

| 1. | n | darkness | 11. | v | ease |
|----|---|----------|-----|---|------|
| 2. | n | limit | 12. | v | extend |
| 3. | n | valley | 13. | v | limit |
| 4. | adj | dull | 14. | v | sit (sat) |
| 5. | adj | obedient | 15. | v | spin (spun) |
| 6. | adj | successful | 16. | v | spread (spread) |
| 7. | adj | thankful | 17. | pre | along |
| 8. | v | appear | 18. | con | even though |
| 9. | v | argue | 19. | adv | eventually |
| 10. | v | avoid | 20. | adv | suddenly |

## B1. Months of the Year

**January** is the 1st month of the year.
**February** is the 2nd month of the year.

**March** is the 3rd month of the year.
**April** is the 4th month of the year.

**May** is the 5th month of the year.
**June** is the 6th month of the year.

## B2. Months of the Year

**July** is the 7th month of the year.
**August** is the 8th month of the year.

**September** is the 9th month of the year.
**October** is the 10th month of the year.

**November** is the 11th month of the year.
**December** is the 12th month of the year.

## B3. Expressing **Partial Dates**

I was born **in** May.
I was born (**on**) May first.
I was born (**on**) the first of May.
I was born **on** the first.

He died **in** June.
He died (**on**) June third.
He died (**on**) the third of June.
He died **on** the third.

**B3**

*A **complete date** consists of the day, month and year. A **partial date** has one or two of them missing.*

## B4. Expressing Full Dates:

(3/5/1980)

I was born (on) **March (the) fifth,**
nineteen (hundred and) eighty.
or
I was born (on) **the fifth of March,**
ninteen (hundred and) eighty.

## B5. Expressing Full Dates:

(1/10/2002)

I started college (on) **January (the) tenth,**
two thousand (and) two.
or
I started college (on) **the tenth of January,**
two thousand (and) two.

## B6. Expressing Full Dates:

(11/14/1799)

He died (on) **November (the) fourteenth,**
seventeen (hundred and) ninety-nine.
or
I was born (on) **the fourteenth of November,**
seventeen (hundred and) ninety-nine.

## B7. List of Irregular Verbs

How far **did** you **run?**
I **ran** ten miles.

**Did** you **see** any houses?
I **saw** only one house.

**Did** you **seek** refuge there?
Yes, I **sought** refuge there.

**Did** they **set** limits to stay there?
Yes, they **set** a one week limit.

---

### B4 - B6

*Full dates can be expressed with written numbers or with words.*

*When writing **dates** with **numbers**, full dates in English start with the month followed by the day and the year.*

*When expressing **dates** with **words**, there are two ways to express full dates. The article in parenthesis (...) may or may not be omitted.*

## C1. Read and Listen to the story.

George Washington was the first President of the United States between the years of 1789 and 1797. He was born February 22, 1732 and died December 14, 1799. Before George Washington became President, he was a tobacco farmer and a soldier in the Continental Army. He became a general in the American Revolution from 1775 to 1783.

Washington married Martha Curtis, a wealthy widow, on January 6, 1759. George and his wife remained married until his death. George Washington fell ill on Thursday December 12, 1799 and died a couple of days later on November 14, 1799. He was 67 years old when he died. His funeral was held on December 18, 1799 at Mount Vernon, near Alexandria, Virginia. He is considered the "Father of the Country".

## C2. Read and Listen to the dialog.

**Who was the first President of the United States?**
The first President of the United States was George Washington.

**When was he President of the United States?**
He was President of the United States between 1789 and 1797.

**What did he do before becoming President of the United States?**
He was a tobacco farmer and a soldier in the Continental Army.

**When did he become a general in the Army?**
He became a general during the War of Independence.

**How long did the War of Independence last?**
It lasted seven years, from 1776 until 1783.

**D1.** Ray (be born) - 5/10/1932 (1934)

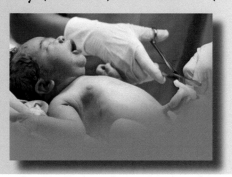

*What date was Ray born?*
He was born on 5/10/1932.

*Were you born before him?*
No, he was born before I was.

*What year were you born?*
I was born 2 years later in 1934.

**D2.** Pat (graduate) - 6/1/1958 (1962)

*What date did Jennifer graduate?*
She graduated on 6/1/1958.

*Did you graduate before her?*
No, she graduated before I did.

*What year did you graduate?*
I graduated 4 years later in 1962.

**D3.** Sam (find a job) - 9/9/1954 (1955)

*What date did Sam find a job?*
He found a job on 9/9/1954.

*Did you find a job before him?*
No, he found a job before I did.

*What year did you find a job?*
I found a job 1 year later in 1955.

**D4.** they (marry) - 2/14/1965 (1964)

*What date did they get married?*
They got married on 2/14/1965.

*Did you get married before them?*
Yes, I got married before they did.

*What year did you get married?*
I got married one year earlier in 1964.

## Verb "to hold"

1. **Hold on** for a moment.
2. **Hold on** to the rope.
3. The crisis **holds down** the prices.
4. They **held up** the bank.
5. The police **held back** the crowd.
6. He is **holding back** something.

## Verb "to agree"

1. We **agreed on** the plan.
2. John did not a**gree with** me.
3. I didn't **agree to** all the details.

**Phrasal verbs** or **prepositional verbs** are verbs followed by a preposition or an adverb. When the verb is followed by a preposition or adverb, the verb acquires a different meaning from the original meaning. When the object of the phrasal verb is a direct object pronoun, the pronoun is placed between the verb and the preposition.

For the English audio pronunciations and written native language translations of **section E,** please go to:

## www.basicesl.com

**Hold on** to the rope.

**We agreed on** the plan.

End of the **oral exercises** for lesson 9.

**You can find additional exercises in sections D, F & G at Basic ESL Online.**

Please continue with the **written exercises** for this lesson in **section H.**

**Lesson 9**

## H1. Write the past tense of these irregular verbs.

1. rid _____
2. run _____
3. see _____
4. seek _____
5. set _____
6. sit _____
7. spin _____
8. spread _____

pay _____
meet _____
quit _____
put _____
read _____
ring _____
rise _____
mean _____

## H2. Complete the sentences with the dates in (...).

1. I was born ... (**6/22**)

   *on June twenty-second.*
   *the twenty-second of June.*

2. Pat left ... (**10/1**)

   _____
   _____

3. She returned ... (**12/3**)

   _____
   _____

4. We applied for a job ... (**May**)

   _____

5. We got a job ... (**Monday**)

   _____

## H3. Complete the sentences with the dates in (...).

1. He got sick (**5 / 5 / 2005**)    *on May fifth, two thousand and five.*

2. I went to college (**1 /13 / 1980**) _____

   _____

3. He became King (**3 / 3 / 1320**) _____

   _____

4. Sue got married (**2 / 14 / 1830**) _____

   _____

5. Washington fell ill (**12 / 12 / 79**) _____

   _____

6. My mom died (**6 / 6 / 2011**) _____

   _____

## H4. Ask the questions corresponding to these answers.

1. Your birthday is **next Tuesday**.    *What day is your birthday?*

2. Today is **May 1st**. _____

3. **Tony's** birthday was yesterday. _____

4. His dad gave him **gifts?** _____

5. The gifts were **expensive**. _____

6. Tony got **5** gifts. _____

7. The party began at **3:00**. _____

8. It lasted **four hours**. _____

9. **Tony** felt very happy. _____

10. Tony also felt **very tired**. _____

11. He arrived home **very late**. _____

## H5. Answer the questions with pronouns.

1. Did **Henry** read the **books**?

   *Yes, **he** read **them**.*

2. Did you sit on the bed?

   _____

3. Did **Frank** set the tables?

   _____

4. Did **Susan** pay her debts?

   _____

5. Did you see **Mary**?

   _____

6. Did she get rid of **David**?

   _____

7. Did **Marilyn** seek help?

   _____

8. Did the you wake up the boys?

   _____

9. Did the lady keep the ring?

   _____

10. Did **Cynthia** lose her leg?

    _____

11. Did you spread the blankets?

    _____

## H6. Answer the questions.

George Washington was the first President of the United States between the years of 1789 and 1797. Before George Washington became President, he was a a soldier in the Continental Army. He became a general in the war of Independence from 1775 to 1783.

Washington married Martha Curtis, on January 6, 1759. George and his wife remained married until his death in 1979 at the age of 67.

1. *Who is George Washington?*

   _____

2. *How long was he President?*

   _____

3. *What was he before becoming President?*

   _____

4. *When did the war on Independence end?*

   _____

5. *Whom did Washington marry?*

   _____

6. *How old was he when he died?*

   _____

## H7. Follow the example.

| | | | | |
|---|---|---|---|---|
| 1. I get up at 3:00 ... *(am)* | at night | at noon | in the afternoon | in the morning |
| 2. Day after Wednesday | Tuesday | Friday | Thursday | Sunday |
| 3. I have lunch at .... | night | noon | morning | evening |
| 4. A year has .... weeks | 50 | 51 | 52 | 53 |
| 5. The shortest month | April | May | January | February |
| 6. The first day of the week | Saturday | Sunday | Monday | Tuesday |

## H8. Follow the example.

1. I know your daughter. _____ is very pretty.      Her, Hers, **She**

2. _____ name is Cecilia.      Her, Hers, She

3. I met _____in one of my vacations in Europe.      her, hers, she

4. I studied in England with _____ nephew.      her, hers, she

5. Cecilia is coming later _____ noon.      on, in, at

6. Her parents are coming also later _____ the evening.      on, in, at

7. They have to leave by 10:00 _____ night.      on, in, at

8. Tony _____ to come also.      want, wants, to want

9. He did not _____ to come last year.      want, wants, to want

10. He can't _____ the next year either.      come, comes, came

11. Tony's nieces may come instead.  I like _____.      they, them, him

12. _____ are my best friends.      They, Them, He

# Chapter 4

# The Weather

# What to do in each section of every lesson...

## A - Vocabulary Study

Section A includes the vocabulary that will be used throughout the lesson. Learning new vocabulary is basic to learning a new language.

**Read** the vocabulary several times.
If you are on Basic ESL Online:
**Listen** to the **English audio pronunciation**.
**View** the **native language translations** of the vocabulary.

Listen and read the vocabulary until you can understand the vocabulary without looking at the words.

## B - Sentence Structure

Section B teaches students basic English sentences using the vocabulary in section A.

**Read** and **study** the sentences.
If you are on Basic ESL Online:
**Listen** to the **English audio pronunciation**.
**View** the **native language translations** of the sentences.
**View** the **grammar concepts** by clicking on the **information button**  .

Repeat the sentences as many times as needed.
Continue to the next section once you can **understand** the sentences without looking at them.

## C - Listening Exercises

**Read** the story or dialog several times.
If you are on Basic ESL Online, **listen** to the story or dialog while reading it several times.

Once you are familiar with the story or dialog, try to see if you can **understand** it by only listening without reading.

## D - Conversation Exercises

**Read** the conversation dialogs several times.
If you are on Basic ESL Online, **listen** to the dialogs until you can understand them without looking at them.

Finally, try to **speak** the conversation dialogs by only looking at the pictures and key words.

## E - Common Phrases

Many of the **common phrases** that are presented in this section are frequently used by the native English speakers in their everyday life.

**Read** the common phrases several times.
If you are on Basic ESL Online, **listen** to the common phrases while reading. **Listen** as many times as needed until you can understand the common phrases without looking at the sentences.

## H - Written Exercises

The written exercises provide an opportunity to test what you learned in the lesson. You can never be sure of knowing something unless you can put it in writing.

You can check your answers by going to the **Answer Key Section** in the back of the workbook.

For information regarding **Basic ESL Online,** please visit **www.basicesl.com.**
Audio Pronunciaton of English & Native Language Translations.

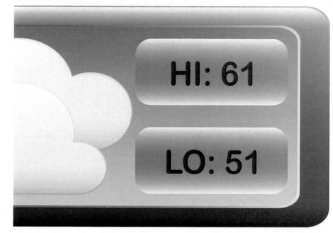

HI: 61

LO: 51

# Lesson #10

# The Weather

## Index

## Audio & Translations

**English Audio available online for sections A-E.**

**Translations in various Languages available online for Sections A, B, and E.**

## www.BasicESL.com

**1.** spring

**2.** summer

**3.** fall (*autumn*)

**4.** winter

**5.** cold weather

**6.** hot weather

**7.** to freeze

**8.** to rain

**9.** to drizzle

**10.** to snow

**11.** to hail

**12.** fog

**13.** nice weather

**14.** sunny weather

**15.** hazy sunshine

**16.** cloudy weather

**17.** smog

**18.** cloud

## Vocabulary Study: Other Vocabulary

| | | | | | |
|---|---|---|---|---|---|
| 1. | n | average | 11. | n | sky |
| 2. | n | chance | 12. | n | wind |
| 3. | n | climate | 13. | adj | inland |
| 4. | n | coast | 14. | adj | mild |
| 5. | n | condition | 15. | v | depend |
| 6. | n | cool | 16. | v | help |
| 7. | n | degree | 17. | v | notice |
| 8. | n | front | 18. | v | vary |
| 9. | n | mid-morning | 19. | adv | how close |
| 10. | n | ocean | 20. | pre | throughout |

For the audio pronunciations and written translations of **Sections A and B,** please go to:

## www.basicesl.com

## Vocabulary Study: Other Vocabulary

| | | | | | |
|---|---|---|---|---|---|
| 1. | n | patch | 11. | adj | rainy |
| 2. | n | showers | 12. | adj | slight |
| 3. | n | visibility | 13. | v | blow (blew) |
| 4. | adj | chilly | 14. | v | draw (drew) |
| 5. | adj | clear | 15. | v | drop |
| 6. | adj | cloudy | 16. | v | hinder |
| 7. | adj | distinct | 17. | con | due to |
| 8. | adj | foggy | 18. | adv | frequently |
| 9. | adj | hazy | 19. | adv | mostly |
| 10. | adj | humid | 20. | adv | partly |

## B1. Expressing Weather Conditions

**ℹ**

**What is the weather like** in winter?
It usually rains and snows.
Last year it rained and snowed a lot.

**How is the weather** in spring?
It usually drizzles and hails.
Yesterday it drizzled and hailed a lot.

**What is the weather like** in July?
It is usually hot and humid.
Last year it was also foggy.

### B1

*There are two ways to inquire about the weather:*

1. *"**What** is the weather **like** in April?"*

2. *"**How** is the weather in April?"*

## B2. Indefinite Time Adverbs

**ℹ**

They **always** walk in the rain.
It is **always** raining in February.

It is **seldom** cold in April.
We **seldom** wear a jacket in May.

It **usually** snows in the winter.
It **hardly** snows in March.

It **never** hails in spring.
It is **never** too cold.

### B2 - B3

*An adverb is a word used to qualify or describe the action of the verb. Adverbs of time give information about when, how long, and how often the action of the verb is taking place. There are two types of time adverbs: definite and indefinite.*

*Indefinite time adverbs don't indicate a specific time. Their position is before the verb, except with the verb "to be".*

*Definite time adverbs usually go after the verb.*

## B3. Definite and Indefinite Time Adverbs

**ℹ**

I **rarely** talk to him.
I talked to him only **once**.

We **constantly** eat fish.
We didn't eat fish **yesterday**.

They **often** forget many things.
They **still** remember your name.

Yesterday Fred got up **late**.
He **generally** gets up at 7:00.

## B4. Definite and Indefinite Time Adverbs

It **hardly** snows in May **now**.
It used to snow in May **before**.

I **frequently** swim in the lake.
I may swim there **tomorrow**.

Did you **ever** smoke in college?
Jane **still** smokes once in a while.

Mike is not going to college **yet**.
Carol might go to college **soon**.

## B5. List of Irregular Verbs

**Did** you **say** that I was sick?
 Yes, I **said** that you were sick.

When **did** you **sell** your house?
 I **sold** it two years ago.

How **did** Jane **send** the letters?
 She **sent** them by express mail.

**Did** the police **shoot** Mark?
 Yes, it **shot** him. He tried to flee.

## B6. List of Irregular Verbs

When **did** you **know** that?
 I **knew** that yesterday.

**Did** Henry **lend** you money?
 Yes, he **lent** me money.

**Did** her sister **shed** any tears?
 Yes, she **shed** some tears.

At what time **did** the star **shine**?
 It **shone** at midnight.

## C1. Read and Listen to the story.

The United States is a big country with a large variety of climate conditions, depending on the location inside the country. Oregon is a beautiful state with a rainy season lasting until March. In the summer months there is a high temperature of 85 degrees and an average low temperature of 40 degrees.

The climate in California varies depending on how close you are to the ocean. Along the coastal areas, the ocean helps to keep the summers cool and the winters warm. Northern California usually receives more rain than Southern California. The inland cities in Southern California can be really hot and dry in the summer. However, in the winter the weather can be mild and warm.

## C2. Read and Listen to the story.

The state of Vermont is located in the northeast of the United States. For the most part, summers in Vermont are usually mild and the winters are very cold. It snows frequently during the winter months. Freezing temperatures are very common. Vermont is one of the few states with four distinct seasons: winter, spring, summer and fall. That is why Vermont is called "the four season state".

Florida is located in the southeast of the United States. It has a rainy season from June to September. It is very hot in the summer, but the winters are very mild. This is why it draws many retired people to its cities due to its warm climate in the winter months. Florida has a dry season during the months of October and May.

**D1.** very hot / 85 degrees

*What is the weather going to be today?*
It is going to be very hot.

*How hot is it going to be?*
It is going to be 85 degrees.

*What was the weather like yesterday?*
It was very hot also.

**D2.** rain (heavily) / 10" sq ft

*What is the weather going to be today?*
It is going to rain heavily.

*How heavily is it going to rain?*
It is going to rain 10" per square foot.

*What was the weather like yesterday?*
It rained a lot also.

**D3.** snow (a lot) / 1'

*What is the weather going to be today?*
It is going to snow a lot.

*How much is it going to snow?*
It is going to snow up to 1' (foot).

*What was the weather like yesterday?*
It snowed a lot also.

**D4.** freeze / -10 degrees

*What is the weather going to be today?*
It is going to be freezing.

*How low is the temperature going to be?*
It is going to be ten degrees below zero.

*What was the weather like yesterday?*
It was freezing also.

## Verb "to run"

1. Did he **run over** the dog?
2. We **ran across** Mark yesterday.
3. The girl **ran away** from home.
4. Soon she **ran out** of money.
5. An old friend **ran into** her yesterday.
6. She is **running up** many debts.

## Verb "to keep"

1. I cannot **keep up** with him.
2. I don't want to **keep on** fighting.
3. **Keep off** this property.

**Phrasal verbs** or **prepositional verbs** are verbs followed by a preposition or an adverb. When the verb is followed by a preposition or adverb, the verb acquires a different meaning from the original meaning. When the object of the phrasal verb is a direct object pronoun, the pronoun is placed between the verb and the preposition.

For the English audio pronunciations and written native language translations of **section E,** please go to:

# www.basicesl.com

I cannot **keep up** with him.

End of the **oral exercises** for lesson 10.

**You can find additional exercises in sections D, F & G at Basic ESL Online.**

Please continue with the **written exercises** for this lesson in **section H.**

Lesson

**10**

**H1.** Write the past tense of these irregular verbs.

| | | | |
|---|---|---|---|
| 1. | lie | _____ | rid _____ |
| 2. | ride | _____ | run _____ |
| 3. | say | _____ | see _____ |
| 4. | sell | _____ | seek _____ |
| 5. | send | _____ | set _____ |
| 6. | shoot | _____ | sit _____ |
| 7. | shed | _____ | spin _____ |
| 8. | shine | _____ | spread _____ |

**H2.** **Answer the questions:** How is the weather today? **and** How was the weather yesterday?

| | | | |
|---|---|---|---|
| 1. | cold | *It is very cold today.* | *It was very cold yesterday.* |
| 2. | to rain | _____ | _____ |
| 3. | sunny | _____ | _____ |
| 4. | hot | _____ | _____ |
| 5. | to snow | _____ | _____ |
| 6. | foggy | _____ | _____ |
| 7. | to drizzle | _____ | _____ |
| 8. | freezing | _____ | _____ |
| 9. | to hail | _____ | _____ |

## H3. Place the definite or indefinite adverb in the right place.

| | | | |
|---|---|---|---|
| 1. | always | I get up early. | *I always get up early.* |
| 2. | always | I am there at noon. | _____ |
| 3. | late | He came to school. | _____ |
| 4. | seldom | He is wrong. | _____ |
| 5. | today | There is no class. | _____ |
| 6. | seldom | He studies at home. | _____ |
| 7. | ever | Did you say bad words? | _____ |
| 8. | usually | We don't say them. | _____ |
| 9. | usually | He is in his room. | _____ |
| 10. | now | I am not working. | _____ |
| 11. | often | Greg sits on that chair. | _____ |
| 12. | often | He is tired. | _____ |
| 13. | early | John didn't come. | _____ |
| 14. | rarely | He comes on Tuesdays. | _____ |
| 15. | rarely | He is here on Sundays. | _____ |
| 16. | still | We work on here. | _____ |
| 17. | still | We are at lunch. | _____ |
| 18. | once | He saw his uncles. | _____ |
| 19. | hardly | He knows them. | _____ |
| 20. | yesterday | They were here. | _____ |
| 21. | soon | She plans to come. | _____ |
| 22. | twice | She promised it. | _____ |
| 23. | generally | Henry cooks on Sunday. | _____ |
| 24. | generally | Mom is busy. | _____ |
| 25. | still | I am sick in bed. | _____ |
| 26. | yet | I'm not well. | _____ |

## H4. Replace the object nouns with pronouns.

1. He kept apart the boys.                    *He kept **them** apart.*
2. Germany took over France.                  _____
3. The teachers break up the fights.          _____
4. Don't tear up the old record.              _____
5. Please, turn on the lights.                _____
6. Throw away the old sandals.                _____
7. Don't give away the new shirt.             _____
8. Don't hang up the phone yet.               _____

## H5. Use of the auxiliary verbs *do, does* and *did* for emphasis.

1. I **saw** an elephant in the river.        *I **did see** an elephant in the river.*
2. They **ran** ten miles.                    _____
3. We **sat** on the snow for a while.        _____
4. You **sell** cars for John.                _____
5. It **stopped** suddenly.                   _____
6. She **rides** the train to work.           _____
7. Tony **meant** that.                        _____
8. We **lent** you $1,000.                    _____

## H6. Make correct sentences using the correct form of the verb.

1. August-the-in-be-how-weather?             *How is the weather in August?*
2. it-sell-he-yesterday.                      _____
3. wear-seldom-she-sandals.                   _____
4. can-hot-be-weather.                        _____
5. still-in-be-February-cold-it.              _____
6. like-what-now-weather-be?                  _____
7. shoot-they-yesterday-him.                  _____

## H7. Complete with possessive adjectives or pronouns.

|     | my | yours |
| --- | --- | --- |
| 1. I don't have …watch and you don't have … . | _____ | _____ |
| 2. Greg wears … shoes.  I wear ….. . | _____ | _____ |
| 3. Carol spends … money and we spend …. … . | _____ | _____ |
| 4. We like … yellow car. Carol likes ….. . | _____ | _____ |
| 5. Carol drives … car.  We drive … . | _____ | _____ |
| 6. I clean … own plate.  Do they clean  … ? | _____ | _____ |
| 7. No, they don't clean …plates.  They  clean …rooms. | _____ | _____ |
| 8. Jim and Hansel wear … own caps.   I wear ….own also. | _____ | _____ |
| 9. Mary and I wear … own gloves. These gloves are … . | _____ | _____ |

## H8. Answer the questions.

United States is a big country with a large variety of climate conditions. Oregon is a beautiful state with a rainy season lasting until March. In the summer months there is a high average temperature of 85 degrees.

The climate in California varies depending on how close you are to the ocean. Along the coastal areas, the summers are cooler than in the inland areas. Northern California receives much more rain than Southern California.

1. *What is the weather like in the United States?*

_____

2. *What is Oregon like?*

_____

3. *When does the rainy season end in Oregon?*

_____

4. *What is the average temperature in the summer?*

_____

5. *On what does the climate in California depend?*

_____

6. *What is the summer weather like in the inland areas?*

_____

_____

# Lesson #11

## Natural Disaster

## Index

## Audio & Translations

**English Audio available online for sections A-E.**

**Translations in various Languages available online for Sections A, B, and E.**

**www.BasicESL.com**

**1.** tornado

**2.** storm

**3.** blizzard

**4.** fire

**5.** earthquake

**6.** avalanche

**7.** flood

**8.** hurricane

**9.** lightning

**10.** thunder

**11.** drought

**12.** volcano

## Vocabulary Study: Other Vocabulary

| | | | | | |
|---|---|---|---|---|---|
| 1. | n | anniversary | 11. | adj | nasty |
| 2. | n | breeze | 12. | adj | windy |
| 3. | n | cruise | 13. | v | board |
| 4. | n | deck | 14. | v | celebrate |
| 5. | n | sea | 15. | v | clear |
| 6. | n | ship | 16. | v | decide |
| 7. | n | wave | 17. | v | forget (forgot) |
| 8. | n | wedding | 18. | v | get scared |
| 9. | adj | calm | 19. | v | see (saw) |
| 10. | adj | clear | 20. | v | shine (shone) |

For the audio pronunciations and written translations of **Sections A and B,** please go to:

**www.basicesl.com**

## Vocabulary Study: Other Vocabulary

| | | | | | |
|---|---|---|---|---|---|
| 1. | n | aftershocks | 11. | v | break out |
| 2. | n | fire | 12. | v | burn (burnt*) |
| 3. | n | force | 13. | v | collapse |
| 4. | n | line | 14. | v | damage |
| 5. | n | pipe | 15. | v | devastate |
| 6. | n | scale | 16. | v | occur |
| 7. | n | witness | 17. | v | relax |
| 8. | adj | homeless | 18. | v | strike (struck) |
| 9. | adj | known | 19. | con | among |
| 10. | adj | severe | 20. | adv | perhaps |

## B1. Indefinite Pronouns

| | | |
|---|---|---|
| A | I saw **somebody**. |
| N | I didn't see **anybody**. |
| A | We spoke to **someone**. |
| N | We didn't speak to **anyone**. |
| A | She noticed **something**. |
| N | She didn't notice **anything**. |
| A | They were **somewhere**. |
| N | They weren't **anywhere**. |

## B2. Indefinite Pronouns

Did **both of them** quit the job?
No, **neither** of them quit it.

Did **all of them** approve the plans?
No, **none** of them approved them.

Did **something** go wrong?
No, **nothing** went wrong.

Did **someone** raise any objection?
No, **no one** raised any objection.

## B3. Indefinite Pronouns

Does she want **something?**
No, she doesn't want **anything**.
No, she wants **nothing**.

Is Mike **somewhere?**
No, he isn't **anywhere**.
No, he is **nowhere**.

Did **somebody** scare you?
Yes, **somebody** scared me.
No, **nobody** scared me.

### B1 - B2 - B3

*Indefinite pronouns are words that replace nouns not specified. They can be singular or plural. If singular, the verb form is singular.*

*Some examples of **singular** indefinite pronouns are "little, each, nothing, everyone, much, nobody, etc."*

***Plural** indefinite pronouns are "many, all, few, several, both."*

*Those derived from "**some**" or "**any**" are used the same way as "**they**."*

## B4. Subject and Object Pronouns

Did **the lightning** hit **the woman**?
Yes, **it** hit **her**.

Did **the earthquake** shake **the houses**?
Yes, **it** shook **them**.

Did **the avalanche** bury **your uncle**?
Yes, **it** buried **him**.

Did **the flood** drown **the animals**?
Yes, **it** drowned **them**.

## B5. List of Irregular Verbs

**Did** Mom **shut** all the windows?
Yes, she **shut** all of them.

Where **did** Mary **sing** last week?
She **sang** in the biggest theater.

**Did** you **speak** with anybody?
Yes, I **spoke** with someone.

Whose clothes **did** the dryer **shrink**?
It **shrank** my brother's clothes.

## B6. List of Irregular Verbs

How fast did you **speed**?
I **sped** at 100 miles an hour.

Did they **slide** down the hill?
Yes, they **slid** down the hill.

How much money did we **spend**?
We **spent** $500.

How long did the children **sleep**?
They **slept** five hours straight.

## C1. Read and Listen to the dialog.

Tony was born in 1935 and Alice three years later. They got married on June 1st, 1968. Last month they celebrated their 25th wedding anniversary. They decided to take a three day cruise to Acapulco. They boarded the ship in the evening. The first night the weather was nice. People were relaxing on the deck of the boat and enjoying the cool breeze of the sea.

On the second day the weather changed for the worse. The sky became dark and cloudy. It started to rain heavily. The temperature dropped several degrees. People started to feel cold. It was very windy. The waves grew bigger and bigger. When they saw the lightning and heard the thunder, my parents got really scared. The storm lasted 7 hours. The next day the fog cleared and they could see the sun shining again. They never forgot that trip to Acapulco by boat.

## C2. Read and Listen to the dialog.

**What year was Tony born?**
He was born in 1945.

**When was his wife born?**
She was born three years later.

**When did they get married?**
They got married in 1968.

**In what month was the wedding?**
It was in the month of January.

**Do they celebrate that day?**
Yes, they do.

**When was their 25th anniversary?**
It was last month.

**How did they celebrate it?**
They celebrated it with a cruise.

**Where did they go?**
They went to Acapulco.

**When did they board the ship?**
They boarded it in the evening.

**How was the weather?**
It was very nice the first night.

**D1.** you (blow up) / gate

*What did you see yesterday?*
I saw a storm and a gate.

*Do storms blow up gates?*
Sometimes they do.
A storm seldom blows up a gate.
Yesterday, however, it blew up the gate.

**D2.** Mark (reach) / roof

*What did Mark see yesterday?*
He saw a flood and a roof.

*Do floods reach the roofs?*
Sometimes they do.
A flood seldom reaches the roof.
Yesterday, however, it reached the roof.

**D3.** boys (strike) / church

*What did the boys see yesterday?*
They saw lightning and a church.

*Does lightning strike churches?*
Sometimes they do.
Lightning seldom strikes a church.
Yesterday, however, it struck the church.

**D4.** Sara (cover) / village

*What did Sara see yesterday?*
She saw an avalanche and a village.

*Do avalanches cover villages?*
Sometimes they do.
Avalanches seldom cover a village.
Yesterday, however, it covered a village.

## Verb "to turn"

1. **Turn on** all the lights but one.
2. **Turn off** the water.
3. Dad **turned in** his son to the police.
4. Why did you **turn down** the offer?
5. It **turned out** to be false.
6. The document **turned up** in the attic.

## Verb "to do"

1. This has nothing **to do with** me.
2. They **did away** with that holiday.
3. I will have **to do without** you.

> **Phrasal verbs** or **prepositional verbs** are verbs followed by a preposition or an adverb. When the verb is followed by a preposition or adverb, the verb acquires a different meaning from the original meaning. When the object of the phrasal verb is a direct object pronoun, the pronoun is placed between the verb and the preposition.

For the English audio pronunciations and written native language translations of **section E,** please go to:

# www.basicesl.com

**Turn on** the light.

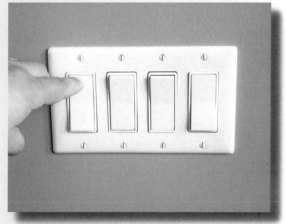

**Turn off** all the lights but one.

End of the **oral exercises** for lesson 11.
**You can find additional exercises in sections D, F & G at Basic ESL Online.**

Please continue with the **written exercises** for this lesson in **section H.**

## H1. Write the past tense of these irregular verbs.

| 1. | shrink | _____ | shake | _____ |
|----|--------|-----------|-------|-----------|
| 2. | shut   | _____ | lend  | _____ |
| 3. | sing   | _____ | say   | _____ |
| 4. | sleep  | _____ | sell  | _____ |
| 5. | slide  | _____ | send  | _____ |
| 6. | speak  | _____ | shoot | _____ |
| 7. | speed  | _____ | shed  | _____ |
| 8. | spend  | _____ | shine | _____ |

## H2. Write the opposite.

| 1. | somebody    | _____ | everybody | _____ |
|----|-------------|-----------|-----------|-----------|
| 2. | someone     | _____ | everyone  | _____ |
| 3. | something   | _____ | near      | _____ |
| 4. | somewhere   | _____ | more      | _____ |
| 5. | anyone      | _____ | a lot     | _____ |
| 6. | anybody     | _____ | many      | _____ |
| 7. | both of them| _____ | far       | _____ |
| 8. | all of them | _____ | better    | _____ |
| 9. | anything    | _____ | most      | _____ |

## H3. Answer the questions with object pronouns.

1. Did **Tony** lend the **money**?      *Yes, **he** lent **it**.*

2. Did John sell the houses? _____

3. Did Mary speak to the girls? _____

4. Did the boys sit on the table? _____

5. Did the group ride the bus? _____

6. Did the men steal the money? _____

7. Did you sweep the floors? _____

8. Did the earthquake shake the city? _____

9. Did the lightning hit the women? _____

10. Did the children sleep on the floor? _____

11. Did Mary sing that song? _____

12. Did Paul spend all the money? _____

13. Did Joe and Ann send the gift? _____

14. Did Lucy shed tears? _____

## H4. Say the same thing in a different way.

1. He didn't **drink any** milk.      *He **drank no** milk.*

2. We didn't **say any** words. _____

3. Jane didn't **sell any** houses. _____

4. Carol didn't **sing any** songs. _____

5. Mom didn't **open any** doors. _____

6. Henry didn't **hear anything**. _____

7. Fred didn't **know any** answers. _____

8. We didn't **eat any** mushrooms. _____

## H5. Answer the questions.

1. Did you see **somebody**?      *No, I didn't see **anybody**.*
     *No, I saw **nobody**.*

2. Did the police shoot **someone**? _____

3. Did you get **something**? _____

4. Did he say **some words**? _____

5. Was he **somewhere**? _____

6. Did the army kill **everybody**? _____

## H6. Select the correct answer.

*Because of the …*

| | | | | |
|---|---|---|---|---|
| 1. Why were you completely wet? | <u>F</u> | **A** | earthquake |
| 2. Why do the children have burns? | _____ | **B** | tornado |
| 3. Why couldn't you see the road? | _____ | **C** | flood |
| 4. Why was the whole family at the beach? | _____ | **D** | thunder |
| 5. Why did the girl cover her ears? | _____ | **E** | fire |
| 6. Why are you wearing a heavy sweater? | _____ | **F** | rain |
| 7. Why are they skiing on the mountain? | _____ | **G** | cold weather |
| 8. Why are there houses without roofs? | _____ | **H** | fog |
| 9. Why is the carpet soaked with water? | _____ | **I** | snow |
| 10. Why is the car on top of that tree? | _____ | **J** | hot weather |
| 11. Why did the buildings fall down? | _____ | **K** | hurricane |

## H7. Answer the following questions.

Tony was born in 1935 and Alice three years later. They got married on June 1st, 1968. Last month they celebrated their 25th wedding anniversary. They decided to take a three day cruise to Acapulco. They boarded the ship in the evening. The first night the weather was nice. People were relaxing on the deck of the boat and enjoying the cool breeze of the sea.

1. *Who is younger, Tony or Alice?*

   _____

2. *What date did they get married?*

   _____

   _____

3. *Why did they take a cruise?*

   _____

   _____

4. *What time did they board the ship?*

   _____

5. *What was the weather like the first night?*

   _____

6. *What were the people doing?*

   _____

   _____

## H8. Choose the correct answer.

1.  He ... to work by car every day.              *went, go, goes, to go*
2.  The children ... go to school walking.        *at night, seldom, late, yesterday*
3.  I feel headaches in the morning ... .         *yesterday, every day, often*
4.  She's ... singing in the choir.               *late, yesterday, still, at noon*
5.  Her daughter does not sing in the choir ... . *rarely, yet, often, badly*
6.  However, she ... sings in the school.         *rarely, often, well, yet*
7.  The food at the restaurant is good. I like ... . *they, them, it, us*
8.  We like Edward. He is staying with ... .      *you, them. us, me*
9.  I didn't ... well last night.                 *to sleep, sleeps, sleep, slept*
10. ... is driving the white car today?           *What, Who, Which, Where*

# Lesson #12

# The Universe

## Index

## Audio & Translations

 English Audio available online for sections A-E.

 Translations in various Languages available online for Sections A, B, and E.

**www.BasicESL.com**

**1.** solar system _____

**2.** star _____

**3.** sun _____

**4.** planet _____

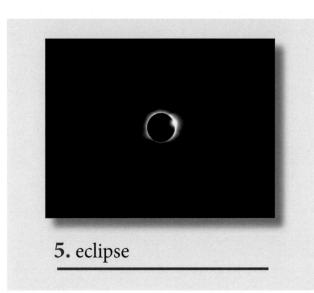

**5.** eclipse _____

**6.** comet _____

**7.** moon

**8.** orbit

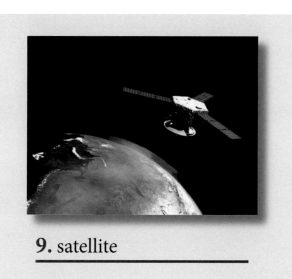

**9.** satellite

**10.** galaxy

**11.** horizon

**12.** rainbow

## Vocabulary Study: Other Vocabulary

| | | | | | | |
|---|---|---|---|---|---|---|
| 1. | n | atmosphere | 11. | n | planet |
| 2. | n | earth | 12. | adj | abundant |
| 3. | n | effect | 13. | adj | complete |
| 4. | n | element | 14. | adj | correct |
| 5. | n | essence | 15. | adj | essential |
| 6. | n | fact | 16. | adj | harmful |
| 7. | n | influence | 17. | adj | right |
| 8. | n | layer | 18. | v | produce |
| 9. | n | orbit | 19. | v | sustain |
| 10. | n | oxygen | 20. | adv | finally |

For the audio pronunciations and written translations of **Sections A and B,** please go to:

**www.basicesl.com**

## Vocabulary Study: Other Vocabulary

| | | | | | | |
|---|---|---|---|---|---|---|
| 1. | n | boat | 11. | adj | tired |
| 2. | n | canal | 12. | v | decide |
| 3. | n | channel | 13. | v | demolish |
| 4. | n | cruise | 14. | v | govern |
| 5. | n | gift | 15. | v | interrupt |
| 6. | n | group | 16. | v | rent |
| 7. | n | tour | 17. | v | rule |
| 8. | n | tourist | 18. | v | strive (strove) |
| 9. | adj | plain | 19. | v | tear (tore) |
| 10. | adj | simple | 20. | v | weep (wept) |

## B1. Tenses: Present (P), Past (Pa), and Future (F)

| | | |
|---|---|---|
| P | I always **eat** lentils. | |
| Pa | I **ate** lentils yesterday. | |
| F | I **will eat** lentils tomorrow. | |
| | | |
| P | We always **travel** by plane. | |
| Pa | We **traveled** by plane yesterday. | |
| F | We **will travel** by plane tomorrow. | |
| | | |
| P | You always **do** homework. | |
| Pa | You **did** homework yesterday. | |
| F | You **will do** homework tomorrow. | |

**B1**

*The simple **future** tense describes actions that will take place in the future. It is formed with the auxiliary verb "**will**" followed by the main verb, which is the same for all subjects.*

## B2. Future Tense: Affirmative and Negative forms

| | |
|---|---|
| A | I **will see** you on Monday. |
| N | I **will not see** you on Tuesday. |
| N | I **won't** see you on Tuesday. |
| | |
| A | They **will come** early. |
| N | They **will not come** late. |
| N | They **won't** come late. |
| | |
| A | He **will approve** this test. |
| N | He **will not approve** the course. |
| N | He **won't** approve the course. |

**B2**

***Negative sentences** in the future tense are formed with the word "**not**" after "**will**." The contraction of "**will not**" is "**won't**".*

## B3. Verb "to be": Future Tense

I **will work** tomorrow.
I **am going to work** tomorrow.

You **will explain** it later.
You **are going to explain** it later.

Dinner **will begin** at 2:00.
Dinner **is going to begin** at two.

She **will pay** the debt soon.
She is **going to pay** the debt soon.

**B3**

*Another way to express future actions is with the verb "to be" + "going to" + main verb.*

## B4. Future Tense: Questions (Q)

**i**

| | |
|---|---|
| | I **will work** tomorrow. |
| Q | **Will I work** tomorrow? |
| | You **will explain** it later. |
| Q | **Will** you **explain** it later? |
| | Dinner **will begin** at 2:00. |
| Q | **Will** dinner **begin** at two? |
| | She **will pay** the debt soon. |
| Q | **Will** she **pay** the debt soon? |

**B4**

*Questions in the future tense are formed with the auxiliary verb "will" at the beginning of the question.*

## B5. Long (L) and Short (S) Answers

**i**

| | |
|---|---|
| | **Will** you **spend** the money? |
| L | Yes, **I will spend** the money. |
| S | Yes, **I will.** |
| | **Will** they **visit** Boston? |
| L | No, they **will not visit** Boston. |
| S | No, they **will not.** |
| | **Will** I **have** time to rest? |
| L | Yes, you **will have** time to rest. |
| S | Yes, you **will.** |

**B5**

*Short answers in the future tense are formed **with the subject** and the auxiliary verb "will."*

## B6. List of Irregular Verbs

**Did** the boy **steal** the money?
Yes, he **stole** the money.

**Did** she **spit** on your face?
Yes, she **spat** on my face.

**Did** he **stick** the knife on the neck?
Yes, he **stuck** it there.

**Did** the water **spring** from a well?
No, it **sprang** from the ground.

## C1. Read and Listen to the Story.

The Earth is the planet where we live. It is located 92 million miles away from the sun. It has a diameter of 7,900 miles. The Earth goes around the sun, producing the calendar year. The orbit around the sun takes an oval form. This means that the distance between the sun and the Earth varies over the course of the year. This fact has an influence in the four seasons of the year.

The planet Earth is the only one known to have life: plant life, animal life and human life. The earth has the essential elements to sustain life: oxygen in the air, abundant water in the oceans, lakes and rivers, a layer of gas in the atmosphere that protects the earth from the harmful effects of the sun, and finally, the correct distance from the sun that gives the right temperature.

## C2. Read and Listen to the Story.

Next year Laura's father will go to Europe. He will visit several countries. He will begin his trip in Germany. From there he will fly to France. After spending one week in Paris, he will take the train to England. He will cross the English Channel by boat. Ten days later he will come back to Paris after visiting London, York and Glasgow. He will rent a car in Paris and will drive south to Spain.

It will take him three days to arrive in Madrid, the capital of Spain. It will be very cold in Madrid during the month of February. This is why he will buy a warm overcoat in one of the best stores of the city. He will pay for it with the American Express card. He also will buy many gifts for his children. At the end of the trip, he will feel tired. He will rest in the plane on his way back to Germany.

**D1.** you (see) / 11:00 am

*What are you going to see?*
I am going to see a comet.

*What time will the comet appear?*
It will appear around 11:00 a.m.

*Will it appear the following day too?*
No, it will not appear again.

**D2.** Lucy (observe) / noon

*What is Lucy going to observe?*
She is going to observe a rainbow.

*What time will the rainbow appear?*
It will appear around noon.

*Will it appear the following day too?*
No, it will not appear again.

**D3.** Henry (watch) / 6:00 pm

*What is Henry going to watch?*
He is going to watch an eclipse.

*What time will the eclipse appear?*
It will appear around 6:00 p.m.

*Will it appear the following day too?*
No, it will not appear again.

**D4.** we (look) / midnight

*What are we going to look at?*
We are going to look at a galaxy.

*What time will the galaxy appear?*
It will appear around midnight.

*Will it appear the following day also?*
No, it will not appear again.

## Verb "to break"

1. The car **broke down** in the freeway.
2. The killer **broke out** of jail.
3. Later he **broke into** my house.
4. Couples **break up** often.
5. America **broke away** from England.

## Verb "to bring"

1. The ice **brought down** the roof.
2. The colors **bring out** the picture.
3. This may **bring about** a war.
4. I **brought** that **up** at the meeting.

**Phrasal verbs** or **prepositional verbs** are verbs followed by a preposition or an adverb. When the verb is followed by a preposition or adverb, the verb acquires a different meaning from the original meaning. When the object of the phrasal verb is a direct object pronoun, the pronoun is placed between the verb and the preposition.

For the English audio pronunciations and written native language translations of **section E,** please go to:

# www.basicesl.com

Later he **broke into** my house

I **brought** that **up** at the meeting.

End of the **oral exercises** for lesson 12.
**You can find additional exercises in sections D, F & G at Basic ESL Online.**

Please continue with the **written exercises** for this lesson in **section H.**

**Lesson 12**

## H1. Write the past tense of these irregular verbs.

| | | | |
|---|---|---|---|
| 1. | steal | _____ | shrink | _____ |
| 2. | spit | _____ | shut | _____ |
| 3. | stick | _____ | sing | _____ |
| 4. | spring | _____ | sink | _____ |
| 5. | stand | _____ | sleep | _____ |
| 6. | strive | _____ | slide | _____ |
| 7. | tear | _____ | speak | _____ |
| 8. | weep | _____ | speed | _____ |

## H2. Change to the future tense.

1. Yesterday I **ate** raisins.     *Tomorrow **I will eat** raisins.*
2. Yesterday **he spat** on the floor. _____
3. Yesterday he **studied** math. _____
4. Yesterday she **rode** the bus. _____
5. Yesterday the school **was** closed. _____
6. Yesterday mom **slept** well. _____
7. Yesterday we **saw** a movie. _____
8. Yesterday they **knelt** in church. _____
9. Yesterday **I spoke** to Edward. _____

## H3. Complete the sentences.

**A**
| | | | |
|---|---|---|---|
| 1. | Every day I | *go* | to the gymnasium. |
| 2. | Today I | *I am going* | to the store. |
| 3. | Yesterday I | *I went* | to John's house. |
| 4. | Tomorrow I | *I will go* | to the mountains. |

**B**
| | | | |
|---|---|---|---|
| 1. | Every day Liz | *works* _____ | in an office. |
| 2. | Today Liz | _____ | at home. |
| 3. | Yesterday Liz | _____ | during the day. |
| 4. | Tomorrow Liz | _____ | at night. |

**C**
| | | | |
|---|---|---|---|
| 1. | Every day my sons | *sweep* _____ | the backyard. |
| 2. | Today my sons | _____ | kitchen. |
| 3. | Yesterday my sons | _____ | the attic. |
| 4. | Tomorrow my sons | _____ | the garden. |

**D**
| | | | |
|---|---|---|---|
| 1. | Every day Fred | *sleeps* _____ | on the bed. |
| 2. | Today Fred | _____ | on the floor. |
| 3. | Yesterday Fred | _____ | in the bus. |
| 4. | Tomorrow Fred | _____ | in the street. |

**E**
| | | | |
|---|---|---|---|
| 1. | Every day Tom | *forgets* _____ | something. |
| 2. | Today Tom | _____ | his birthday. |
| 3. | Yesterday Tom | _____ | his hat. |
| 4. | Tomorrow Tom | _____ | his name probably. |

**F**
| | | | |
|---|---|---|---|
| 1. | Every day they | *steal* _____ | something. |
| 2. | Today they | _____ | food. |
| 3. | Yesterday they | _____ | money. |
| 4. | Tomorrow they | _____ | some clothes. |

## H4. Make the sentence negative.

1. Claire **is working** now.          *Claire is **not** working now.*
2. She **will work** until five.        _____
3. Yesterday she **worked** late.        _____
4. She usually **works** late.          _____
5. Today she **can** leave earlier.        _____
6. She **must** arrive home soon.        _____
7. She **will ride** the bus home.        _____
8. She **may** walk home.              _____

## H5. Change the statements to questions.

1. Claire **is working** now.          ***Is Claire working** now?*
2. She **will work** until five.        _____
3. Yesterday she **worked** late.        _____
4. She usually **works** late.          _____
5. Today she **can** leave earlier.        _____
6. She **must** arrive home soon.        _____
7. She **will ride** the bus home.        _____
8. She **may** walk home now.          _____

## H6. Write the same sentence using *"going to"*.

1. **I will stop** in England.          ***I am going to stop** in England.*
2. We will swim in the river.        _____
3. We will not swim in the lake.        _____
4. Greg will not come with us.        _____
5. The boys will fly to France.        _____
6. The girls will stay home.          _____
7. It will be cold in winter.          _____

## H7. Change *next year* for *last year*.

**Next year** Laura's father **will go** to Europe. He **will visit** several countries. He **will begin** his trip in Germany. From there he **will fly** to France.

After spending one week in Paris, he **will take** the train to England. He **will cross** the English Channel by boat.

Ten days later he **will come back** to Paris after visiting London, York and Glasgow. He **will rent** a car in Paris and **will drive** south to Spain.

It **will take** him three days to arrive in Madrid, the capital of Spain. It **will be** very cold in Madrid during the month of February.

This is why he **will buy** a warm overcoat in one of the best stores of the city. He **will pay** for it with the American Express card.

*Last year* Laura's father **went** to Europe. _____

_____

_____

_____

_____

_____

_____

_____

_____

_____

_____

_____

_____

_____

_____

_____

_____

_____

_____

# Chapter 5
# The World

# What to do in each section of every lesson

## A - Vocabulary Study

Section A includes the vocabulary that will be used throughout the lesson. Learning new vocabulary is basic to learning a new language.

**Read** the vocabulary several times.
If you are on Basic ESL Online:
**Listen** to the **English audio pronunciation**.
**View** the **native language translations** of the vocabulary.

Listen and read the vocabulary until you can understand the vocabulary without looking at the words.

## B - Sentence Structure

Section B teaches students basic English sentences using the vocabulary in section A.

**Read** and **study** the sentences.
If you are on Basic ESL Online:
**Listen** to the **English audio pronunciation**.
**View** the **native language translations** of the sentences.
**View** the **grammar concepts** by clicking on the **information button**  .

Repeat the sentences as many times as needed. Continue to the next section once you can **understand** the sentences without looking at them.

## C - Listening Exercises

**Read** the story or dialog several times.
If you are on Basic ESL Online, **listen** to the story or dialog while reading it several times.

Once you are familiar with the story or dialog, try to see if you can **understand** it by only listening without reading.

## D - Conversation Exercises

**Read** the conversation dialogs several times.
If you are on Basic ESL Online, **listen** to the dialogs until you can understand them without looking at them.

Finally, try to **speak** the conversation dialogs by only looking at the pictures and key words.

## E - Common Phrases

Many of the **common phrases** that are presented in this section are frequently used by the native English speakers in their everyday life.

**Read** the common phrases several times.
If you are on Basic ESL Online, **listen** to the common phrases while reading. **Listen** as many times as needed until you can understand the common phrases without looking at the sentences.

## H - Written Exercises

The written exercises provide an opportunity to test what you learned in the lesson. You can never be sure of knowing something unless you can put it in writing.

You can check your answers by going to the **Answer Key Section** in the back of the workbook**.**

For information regarding **Basic ESL Online,** please visit **www.basicesl.com**.
Audio Pronunciaton of English & Native Language Translations.

# Lesson #13

## The Countries

## Index

## Audio & Translations

**English Audio available online for sections A-E.**

**Translations in various Languages available online for Sections A, B, and E.**

**www.BasicESL.com**

**1.** Europe

**2.** Australia

**3.** North America

**4.** South America

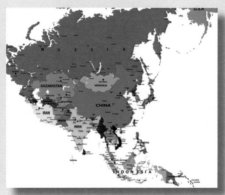

**5.** Asia

**6.** Africa

**7.** United States

**8.** Canada

**9.** Mexico

**10.** Brazil

**11.** Japan

**12.** Iran

**13.** India

**14.** China

**15.** Italy

**16.** Germany

**17.** Spain

**18.** France

## Vocabulary Study: Other Vocabulary

| | | | | | | |
|---|---|---|---|---|---|---|
| 1. | n | billion | 11. | v | contain |
| 2. | n | galaxy | 12. | v | guess |
| 3. | n | other | 13. | v | guide |
| 4. | n | solar | 14. | v | penetrate |
| 5. | n | space | 15. | v | regret |
| 6. | n | system | 16. | v | rest |
| 7. | n | universe | 17. | v | spill |
| 8. | n | whole | 18. | v | yell |
| 9. | v | belong | 19. | pre | beyond |
| 10. | v | comprise | 20. | adv | together |

For the audio pronunciations and written translations of **Sections A and B,** please go to:

**www.basicesl.com**

## Vocabulary Study: Other Vocabulary

| | | | | | | |
|---|---|---|---|---|---|---|
| 1. | n | copper | 11. | v | encourage |
| 2. | n | figure | 12. | v | identify |
| 3. | n | gold | 13. | v | ignore |
| 4. | n | interruption | 14. | v | imagine |
| 5. | n | machine | 15. | v | miss |
| 6. | n | signature | 16. | v | please |
| 7. | n | silver | 17. | v | press |
| 8. | n | stone | 18. | v | release |
| 9. | adj | final | 19. | v | rescue |
| 10. | adj | such | 20. | v | sign |

## B1. Verbs: Tag Questions

| | | |
|---|---|---|
| **Pr** | I **come** from Mexico, **do** I **not**? | |
| | I **do not come** from Brazil, **do** I? | |
| **Pr** | He **goes** to Chile, **does** he **not**? | |
| | He **does not go** to Peru, **does** he? | |
| **Pa** | You **flew** to Australia, **did** you **not**? | |
| | You **did not fly** to Bolivia, **did** you? | |
| **Fu** | Pat **will come** soon, **will** she **not**? | |
| | She **will not come** late, **will** she? | |

## B2. Verbs: Tag Questions

| | | |
|---|---|---|
| **Pr** | We **cook** for you, **do** we **not**? | |
| | We **do not cook** for them, **do** we? | |
| **Pr** | Carol **teaches** math, **does** she **not**? | |
| | Carol **does not teach** art, **does** she? | |
| **Pa** | I **treated** you well, **did** I **not**? | |
| | I **did not treat** you badly, **did** I? | |
| **Fu** | They **will take** the bus, **will** they **not**? | |
| | They **will not take** the train, **will** they? | |

**B1 - B2**

*Tag questions* are questions consisting of two parts, a statement and a question at the end, called a tag question. If the statement is affirmative, the tag question is negative. If the statement is negative, the tag question is affirmative.

## B3. Prepositions at the end of questions.

**What** did you step **on**?
**On what** did you step?

**What** were you thinking (**about**)?
(**About**) what were you thinking?

**Who** (**whom**) did you talk **with**?
**With whom** did you talk?

**Who** (**whom**) did he work **for**?
**For whom** did he work?

**B3 - B4**

*Prepositions* can be at the beginning or at the end of the sentence. Although there are disagreements about whether it is correct to end a sentence with a preposition, it is very common. When the sentence is clear without the preposition at the end, the preposition can be omitted.

## B4. Prepositions at the end of questions.

**What** did they fire Tom **for**?
**For what** did they fire Tom?

**Where** did your parents go (**to**)?
(**To**) **where** did your parents go?

**Who** is she fighting **against**?
**Against whom** is she fighting?

**What** are they thinking (**of**)?
(**Of**) **what** are they thinking?

**B3-B4 (continued)**

## B5. List of Irregular Verbs

Which language course **did** you **take**?
I **took** a French course.

Where **did** they **swim**?
They **swam** in the lake.

What **did** Peter **sweep** the patio with?
He **swept** it with a broom.

**Did** the car **strike** two pedestrians?
Yes, it **struck** them with great force.

## B6. List of Irregular Verbs

**Did** a spider **sting** your leg?
No, probably a bee **stung** me.

That animal **stinks** sometimes.
Yesterday it **stunk** all day.

**Did** they **swear** to tell the truth?
Yes, they **swore** to tell the truth.

Which subjects **did** Mrs. Blair **teach**?
She **taught** music and art.

## C1. Read and Listen to the story.

Last year Richard **went** to Europe. He **visited** several countries. Richard has a friend in Sweden. Her name is Kristy. After visiting her, he began his tour through Europe. From Sweden he **flew** to Greece. After spending one week in Athens, its capital, he **took** the train to Switzerland. Afterwards he **flew** to Hungary, where he **joined** a group of tourists. They **took** a river cruise through several European countries.

Richard **arrived** in Holland five days later, after stopping in several cities along the way. He **spent** two days visiting Amsterdam, its capital. It is famous for its flowers and canals. There he **rented** a car and **drove** to Belgium. It **took** him one day to arrive in Brussels, the capital of Belgium. It is very cold in Brussels during the month of February. This is why he **bought** a heavy sweater in the city. He **felt** tired at the end of the trip. He **rested** in the plane on his way back to United States.

## C2. Read and Listen to the dialog.

*Richard did not go to Russia last year, **did he?***
No, he didn't. He went to Europe.

*He has a friend in Sweden, **does he not?***
Yes, he does. Her name is Kristy.

*They did not travel together in Europe, **did they?***
No, they didn't. She stayed in Sweden.

*He did not fly to Switzerland, **did he?***
No, he didn't. He flew to Greece.

*He and some tourist took a river cruise in Hungary, **did they not?***
Yes, they did. The cruise lasted five days.

**D1.** Mary (come-live) / Yes

***What map is this?***
This is a map of Mexico.

***Mary came from Mexico, didn't she?***
Yes, she did.

***She doesn't live in Mexico now, does she?***
Yes, she does.

**D2.** Roger (come-live) / Yes

***What map is this?***
This is a map of the U.S.A.

***Roger came from the U.S.A., didn't he?***
Yes, he did.

***He doesn't live in the U.S.A. now, does he?***
Yes, he does.

**D3.** ladies (come-live) / Yes

***What map is this?***
This is a map of Japan.

***The ladies came from Japan, didn't they?***
Yes, they did.

***They don't live in Japan now, do they?***
Yes, they do.

**D4.** you (come-live) / Yes

***What map is this?***
This is a map of Spain.

***You came from Spain, didn't you?***
Yes, I did.

***You don't live in Spain now, do you?***
Yes, I do.

## Verb "to pull"

1. They are going **to pull down** the school.
2. **Pull up** your pants, please.
3. I **pulled over** the car on the freeway.
4. **Pull off** your sweater.
5. She is **pulling ahead** of Paul.
6. The mechanic **pulled apart** the pieces.
7. They **pulled through** a bad situation.

**Phrasal verbs** or **prepositional verbs** are verbs followed by a preposition or an adverb. When the verb is followed by a preposition or adverb, the verb acquires a different meaning from the original meaning. When the object of the phrasal verb is a direct object pronoun, the pronoun is placed between the verb and the preposition.

For the English audio pronunciations and written native language translations of **section E,** please go to:

# www.basicesl.com

## Verb "to throw"

1. I feel like **throwing up.**
2. Don't **throw away** any shoes.

I feel like **throwing up.**

End of the **oral exercises** for lesson 13.
**You can find additional exercises in sections D, F & G at Basic ESL Online.**

Please continue with the **written exercises** for this lesson in **section H.**

Lesson **13**

**H1.** Write the past tense of these irregular verbs.

| | | | | |
|---|---|---|---|---|
| 1. | take | _____ | steal | _____ |
| 2. | swim | _____ | spit | _____ |
| 3. | sweep | _____ | stick | _____ |
| 4. | strike | _____ | spring | _____ |
| 5. | sting | _____ | stand | _____ |
| 6. | stinks | _____ | strive | _____ |
| 7. | swear | _____ | tear | _____ |
| 8. | teach | _____ | weep | _____ |

**H2.** Prepositions at the end of questions.

1. **For** what did you do that?      *What did you do that **for**?*

2. **For** whom do you work? _____

3. **With** whom did you go? _____

4. **Against** whom are they fighting? _____

5. **About** what are you talking? _____

6. **Of** what is she thinking? _____

7. **To** where is your aunt going? _____

8. **On** what did she step? _____

## H3. Complete with tag questions in the present tense.

1. Richard **goes** to Europe,      *does he not?*

2. My uncle **doesn't go** to Asia, _____

3. My sister **has** a house there, _____

4. Her nephew **lives** in Sweden, _____

5. He **doesn't live** in Spain, _____

6. I **get up** early in the morning, _____

7. I **don't get up** at noon, _____

## H4. Complete with tag questions in the past tense.

1. Richard **went** to Europe,      *did he not?*

2. My uncle **didn't go** to Asia, _____

3. My sister **had** a house there, _____

4. Her nephew **lived** in Sweden, _____

5. He **did not live** in Spain, _____

6. I **got up** early in the morning, _____

7. I **didn't get** up at noon, _____

## H5. Complete with tag questions in the future tense.

1. Richard **will go** to Europe,      *will he not?*

2. My uncle **will not go** to Asia, _____

3. My sister **will have** a house there, _____

4. Her nephew **will live** in Sweden, _____

5. He **will not live** in Spain, _____

6. I **will get** up early in the morning, _____

7. I **will not get** up at noon, _____

## H6. Follow the example.

1.  you

    **France**

    **You don't come from France, do you?**
    *Yes, I do.*

    **But you don't live in France now, do you?**
    *No, I don't.*

2.  Cecilia & Patty

    **Mexico**

    _____
    _____
    _____
    _____

3.  Keiko & you

    **Japan**

    _____
    _____
    _____
    _____

4.  Kate

    **Spain**

    _____
    _____
    _____
    _____

5.  Carlos

    **Sweden**

    _____
    _____
    _____
    _____

**H7.** Change *last year* for *next year.*

**Last year** Richard **went** to Europe. First he made a visit to a friend in Sweden. From Sweden he **flew** to Greece.

He **spent** one week in Athens, its capital. Then he **took** the train to Switzerland. There he **got on** a bus going to Hungary. Two days later, he **took** a river cruise through several European countries.

Richard **arrived** in Holland five days later. In Holland he **rented** a car and **drove** to Belgium. It **was** very cold in Brussels when he arrived. This is why he **bought** an overcoat in the city.

He **felt** tired at the end of the trip. He **slept** in the plane on his way back to the United States.

*Next year* Richard **will go to** *Europe.* _____

_____

_____

_____

_____

_____

_____

_____

_____

_____

_____

_____

_____

_____

_____

_____

_____

# Lesson #14

# Nationalities

## Index

## Audio & Translations

 English Audio available online for sections A-E.

 Translations in various Languages available online for Sections A, B, and E.

## www.BasicESL.com

**1.** French *(France)*

**2.** Mexican *(Mexico)*

**3.** Italian *(Italy)*

**4.** English *(England)*

**5.** Japanese *(Japan)*

**6.** Chinese *(China)*

**7.** Indian *(India)*

**8.** Russian *(Russia)*

**9.** German *(Germany)*

**10.** Spanish *(Spain)*

**11.** Greek *(Greece)*

**12.** American *(US)*

**13.** Arabic *(Arabia)*

**14.** Peruvian *(Peru)*

**15.** Bolivian *(Bolivia)*

**16.** Egyptian *(Egypt)*

**17.** Guatemalan *(Guatemala)*

**18.** African *(Africa)*

## Vocabulary Study: Other Vocabulary

| | | | | | |
|---|---|---|---|---|---|
| 1. | n | appear | 11. | v | beat (beat) |
| 2. | n | basket | 12. | v | catch (caught) |
| 3. | n | court | 13. | v | declare |
| 4. | n | fine | 14. | v | pay (paid) |
| 5. | n | game | 15. | v | run (ran) |
| 6. | n | goal | 16. | v | score |
| 7. | n | penalty (foul) | 17. | v | shoot (shot) |
| 8. | n | referee | 18. | v | throw (threw) |
| 9. | n | team | 19. | v | tie |
| 10. | adj | tied | 20. | v | win (won) |

For the audio pronunciations and written translations of **Sections A and B,** please go to:

**www.basicesl.com**

## Vocabulary Study: Other Vocabulary

| | | | | | |
|---|---|---|---|---|---|
| 1. | n | loss | | | |
| 2. | n | prize | 11. | v | annoy |
| 3. | adj | brief | 12. | v | convince |
| 4. | adj | optimistic | 13. | v | deny |
| 5. | adj | partial | 14. | v | ignore |
| 6. | adj | pessimistic | 15. | v | meet (met) |
| 7. | adj | responsible | 16. | v | require |
| 8. | adj | silent | 17. | v | score |
| 9. | adj | weary | 18. | v | succeed |
| 10. | adj | wicked | 19. | v | weave (wove) |

## B1. Verb "to be": Tag Questions: Present Tense

I **am** Mexican, **am** I **not**?
I **am not** Mexican, **am** I?

You **are** English, **are** you **not**?
You **are not** English, **are** you?

He **is** Dutch, is he **not**?
He **is not** Dutch, **is** he?

We **are** Polish, **are** we **not**?
We **are not** Polish, **are** we?

**B1 - B2**

*Tag questions with the verb "to be," follow the same rules of the other verbs. If the sentence is affirmative, the tag question is negative. If the sentence is negative, the tag question is affirmative.*

## B2. Tag Questions: Past and Future Tense

I **was** there, **was** I **not**?
I **was not** there, **was** I?

Jane **was** Jewish, **was** she **not**?
Jane **was not** Jewish, **was** she?

Greg **will be** a doctor, **will** he **not**?
Greg **will not be** a doctor, **will** he?

You and I **will be** rich, **will** we **not**?
You and I **will not be** poor, **will** we?

## B3. Modal Verbs: Tag Questions

You **can** do it, **can't** you?
You **cannot** do it, **can** you?

Ann **could** convince him, **couldn't** she?
Ann **couldn't** convince him, **could** she?

Greg **should** be optimistic, **shouldn't** he?
Greg **shouldn't** be pessimistic, **should** he?

You **would help** them, **wouldn't** you?
You **wouldn't help** them, **would** you?

**B3**

*Tag questions with modal verbs are formed by repeating the modal verb in the tag questions.*

## B4. Verb Form Following a Preposition or Adverb

**ℹ**

Don't drink **before** driving.
Be polite **when** talking to someone.

You will succeed **by** working hard.
They will jail you **for** stealing.

Let's talk **about** buying the house.
Don't read **before** going to bed.

I fainted **upon** seeing him.
I always rest **after** running.

**B4**

*The form of the verb after a preposition or an adverb ends in "-ing."*

## B5. List of Irregular Verbs

**Didn't** I **tell** you this many times?
    Yes, you **told** me that 10 times.

Where **did** you **throw** the old clothes?
    I **threw** them in the trash.

What time **did** she **wake up** yesterday?
    She **woke up** in the evening.

What prize **did** you **win** in the lottery?
    I **won** a sports car.

## B6. List of Irregular Verbs

What **did** you **think** about Mary?
    I **thought** she was a nice girl.

What **did** she **wear** during the trip?
    She **wore** jeans and a shirt.

**Did** you **write** these letters?
    Yes, I **wrote** them.

**Did** Jane **weave** her sweater?
    Yes, she **wove** it.

## C1. Read and Listen to the story.

Alex plays basketball at Oceanside High School. He is one of the best players on the team. Last Friday Alex's team had an important game against Irvine High School. At 5:30 pm, the two teams appeared on the basketball court with their own coaches.

At the sound of the referee's whistle, the referee threw the ball in the air. Alex caught the ball and ran several yards dribbling the ball on the floor. Instead of shooting the ball in the basket, he passed the ball to Tony, one of his teammates. Tony tried to score a basket. His opponent pushed him and Tony fell to the floor. The referee blew the whistle and declared a foul against Irvine High School. Tony didn't have a problem scoring the first basket for Oceanside High School.

At the end of the first half, both teams were tied 15 to 15. The second half of the game ended with Oceanside winning over Irvine 40 to 38. They will play again next year.

## C2. Read and Listen to the dialog.

*Tony **is** a better player than Alex, **is** he **not**?*
    No, he **is no**t. Alex is the best player on the team.

*Alex's team **had** an important game last Friday, **did** it **not**?*
    Yes, it **did**. The game started at 5:30 pm.

*The two teams play a basketball game every year, **do** they **not**?*
    Yes, they **do**.

*The referee t**hrew** the ball in the air, **did** he **not**?*
    Yes, he **did** it after blowing the whistle.

*Both teams will play again next year, **will** they **not**?*
    Yes, they **will**, especially if Irvine High School loses the game.

**D1.** Mark / Russia

**Mark is not Russian, is he?**
No, he isn't.

**He is Mexican, is he not?**
Yes, he is.

**So, he comes from Mexico, doesn't he?**
Yes, he does.

**D2.** they / Vietnamese

**They are not Vietnamese, are they?**
No, they aren't.

**They are Chinese, are they not?**
Yes, they are.

**So, they come from China, don't they?**
Yes, they do.

**D3.** Alice / Italian

**Alice is not Italian, is she?**
No, she isn't.

**She is Indian, is she not?**
Yes, she is.

**So, she comes from India, doesn't she?**
Yes, she does.

**D4.** the girls / French

**The girls are not French, are they?**
No, they aren't.

**They are Spanish, are they not?**
Yes, they are.

**So, they come from Spain, don't they?**
Yes, they do.

## Verb "to catch"

1. The young boy is **catching up with** you.
2. McDonald's is **catching on** in Paris.
3. I need **to catch up on** this.

## Verb "to carry"

1. I **carried on** doing the same thing.
2. Don't **carry out** his orders.
3. I **carry through** all my projects.

## Verb "to care"

1. My sister **cares after** the baby.
2. He doesn't **care about** your business.
3. Do you **care for** a drink?

**Phrasal verbs** or **prepositional verbs** are verbs followed by a preposition or an adverb. When the verb is followed by a preposition or adverb, the verb acquires a different meaning from the original meaning. When the object of the phrasal verb is a direct object pronoun, the pronoun is placed between the verb and the preposition.

For the English audio pronunciations and written native language translations of **section E,** please go to:

# www.basicesl.com

My sister **cares after** the baby.

End of the **oral exercises** for lesson 14.
**You can find additional exercises in sections D, F & G at Basic ESL Online.**

Please continue with the **written exercises** for this lesson in **section H**.

Lesson

# 14

## H1. Write the past tense of these irregular verbs.

| | | | | | |
|---|---|---|---|---|---|
| 1. | tell | _____ | swim | _____ |
| 2. | think | _____ | sweep | _____ |
| 3. | throw | _____ | strike | _____ |
| 4. | wake | _____ | sting | _____ |
| 5. | win | _____ | stinks | _____ |
| 6. | wear | _____ | swear | _____ |
| 7. | write | _____ | take | _____ |
| 8. | weave | _____ | teach | _____ |

## H2. Complete with the correct form of the verb.

| | | | |
|---|---|---|---|
| 1. | **study** | You will get better grades by ... more. | *studying* |
| 2. | go | I don't work before ... to bed. | _____ |
| 3. | listen | After ... to John, I think he is right. | _____ |
| 4. | warn | Ed changed his mind, after ... him about the danger. | _____ |
| 5. | answer | Think twice before ... the question. | _____ |
| 6. | close | Lock the door after ... the door. | _____ |
| 7. | speak | Be always polite when .... to someone. | _____ |
| 8. | steal | The police jailed the young man for ... a car. | _____ |
| 9. | travel | I feel very sleepy after ... during the night. | _____ |

## H3. Verb "to be": Complete with tag questions.

1. Albert **is** a student,     *is he not?*

2. Albert **is not** a teacher, _____

3. These boys **are** his cousins, _____

4. These boys **are not** his friends, _____

5. I **am** American, _____

6. I **am not** Chinese, _____

7. You **were** in France yesterday, _____

8. You **were not** in England, _____

9. Monica **was** working in Russia, _____

10. Monica **was not** working in Greece, _____

11. We **will be** doctors, _____

12. We **will not** be nurses. _____

## H4. Modal Verbs: Complete with tag questions.

1. You **can** teach math,     *can't you?*

2. You **cannot** teach physics, _____

3. Tony and Lucy **could** talk to Lydia, _____

4. They **couldn't** talk to Margaret, _____

5. I **should** go to the clinic, _____

6. I **should not** go to work, _____

7. Mary **would** like to be a teacher, _____

8. Mary **would not** like to be a doctor, _____

9. We **must** respect our parents, _____

10. We **must not** insult them, _____

11. Richard **ought** to return home, _____

12. Richard **ought not** to return home, _____

## H5. Complete with the correct prepositions.

1. Put the heavy books … the bottom, together … the heavy ones.    *at / with*
2. Put the pictures … the middle shelf, not … the top shelf.    _____
3. Don't place the books … of the bookcase or … the floor.    _____
4. Look … that picture … the wall. Its size is 10 … 9.    _____
5. Stand … now. Don't lean … the window.    _____
6. I complained … him, but I didn't laugh … him.    _____
7. I seldom get …  … seven o'clock … the morning.    _____
8. I eat … noon and I play … the evening.    _____
9. You generally go … bed … midnight.    _____

## H6. Complete with **they, them, their** or **theirs**

1. Helen and Pat are Mexican. Mexico is … country.    *their*    _____
2. I saw … on … way to Mexico last year.    _____    _____
3. … go to Mexico during … Christmas vacation.    _____    _____
4. My vacations are short.  … are long.    _____    _____
5. During the vacation I spend my money and … spend …    _____    _____
6. I spoke to … yesterday. … are coming back soon.    _____    _____

## H7. Answer the questions with pronouns.

1. Did **the men** bring the **money**?    *Yes, **they did. They** brought **it**.*
2. Did **Henry** choose that **food**?    _____
3. Did **Jane** forgive **Raymond**?    _____
4. Did **Jane** speak to **Susan**?    _____
5. Did the **women** pay their **bills**?    _____
6. Did the **school** tell **Mary** that?    _____
7. Did **Tom** write these **letters**?    _____
8. Did **you** throw away the **shoes**?    _____

## H8. Follow the example.

1.  I / U.S.A.

    **Germany**

    *I am not American, **am I?***
      No, you aren't.
    *I am German, **am I not?***
      Yes, you are.

2.  students / Italy

    **China**

    _____
    _____
    _____
    _____

3.  Henry / Poland

    **Russia**

    _____
    _____
    _____
    _____

4.  women / Holland

    **Japan**

    _____
    _____
    _____
    _____

5.  daughter / France

    **Mexico**

    _____
    _____
    _____
    _____

# Lesson #15

## Geography

## Audio & Translations

 English Audio available online for sections A-E.

 Translations in various Languages available online for Sections A, B, and E.

www.BasicESL.com

**1.** coast

**2.** falls

**3.** iceberg

**4.** ocean

**5.** jungle

**6.** valley

**7.** hill

**8.** lake

**9.** river

**10.** mountain

**11.** island

**12.** peninsula

**13.** bay

**14.** gulf

**15.** gorge

**16.** canyon

**17.** cape

**18.** strait

## Vocabulary Study: Other Vocabulary

| 1. | n | airport | 11. | v | board |
|---|---|---|---|---|---|
| 2. | n | arrival | 12. | v | depart |
| 3. | n | baggage | 13. | v | fasten |
| 4. | n | citizen | 14. | v | greet |
| 5. | n | compartment | 15. | v | indicate |
| 6. | n | departure | 16. | v | land |
| 7. | n | gate | 17. | v | look forward |
| 8. | n | passport | 18. | v | pack |
| 9. | n | stewardess | 19. | v | take off |
| 10. | n | suitcase | 20. | adv | sharp |

For the audio pronunciations and written translations of **Sections A and B,** please go to:

**www.basicesl.com**

## Vocabulary Study: Other Vocabulary

| 1. | n | trap | 11. | adj | uneven |
|---|---|---|---|---|---|
| 2. | n | budget | 12. | adj | witty |
| 3. | n | fine | 13. | v | admire |
| 4. | n | trace | 14. | v | ban |
| 5. | adj | envious | 15. | v | harass |
| 6. | adj | final | 16. | v | hurry |
| 7. | adj | fine | 17. | v | intend |
| 8. | adj | hesitant | 18. | v | pause |
| 9. | adj | sorrowful | 19. | v | pretend |
| 10. | adj | steep | 20. | adv | on time |

## B1. Verbs: Future Tense: Affirmative Contractions

**I will** go to the jungle.
C   **I'll** go to the jungle.

**You will** fly over the ocean.
C   **You'll** fly over the ocean.

**She will** swim in the river.
C   **She'll** swim in the river.

**They will** visit the island.
C   **They'll** visit the island.

**B1 - B2**

*Contractions* in the future tense can be used both in affirmative and negative sentences. In affirmative sentences, *"will"* contracts to *"-ll"* and is attached mainly to the subject pronouns with an apostrophe.

## B2. Verbs: Future Tense: Negative Contractions

I **will not go** to the bay.
C   I **won't go** to the bay.

We **will not approach** the coast.
C   We **won't approach** the coast.

He **will not sail** near the falls.
C   He **won't sail** near the falls.

It **will not work** this time.
C   It **won't work** this time.

**B2 - B3**

*To form negative contractions in the future tense, *"will not"* is changed to *"won't"*.*

## B3. Future Tense: Tag Endings with Contractions

You **will** learn German, **won't** you?
You **won't** learn Arabic, **will** you?

Jane **will** be a dentist, **won't** she?
Jane **won't** be a doctor, **will** she?

**We'll** fly to Italy, **won't** we?
We **won't** fly to Poland, **will** we?

**They'll** spend a week here, **won't** they?
They **won't** spend a month here, **will** they?

## B4. Future Tense: Questions and Answers

|       | **Will he** talk to you later?   |
|-------|----------------------------------|
| **Long**  | Yes, **he'll** talk to me later. |
| **Short** | Yes, he **will**.                |

|       | **Will he** come here?           |
|-------|----------------------------------|
| **Long**  | No, he **won't** come here.      |
| **Short** | No, he **won't**.                |

|       | **Will they** tell us the truth?     |
|-------|--------------------------------------|
| **Long**  | Yes, **they'll** tell us the truth. |
| **Short** | No, they **won't**.                 |

## B5. The adverb "else"

Who **else** is coming?
   My sister is also coming.

What **else** do you want?
I want something **else**.

Who **else** did you speak with?
   I spoke with no one **else**.

Where **else** could Martha be?
   She can't be anywhere **else**.

### B5 - B6

*The adverb **"else"** means **other** or something **different**. It is used with question words like **"who, where, how, what"** or after words beginning with **"some, every, any."***

## B6. The adverb "else"

**Who else** do you miss?
   I miss my **grandparents**.

**What else** did you ask for?
   I asked for a **vacation**.

**Where else** will you go?
   I will go to **Italy**.

**How else** did you feel?
   I felt really **angry**.

## C1. Read and Listen to the story.

July and Ray are American citizens. They're looking forward to their first vacation in England. They plan to visit London where they have some friends. They're German living in London. They already have their passports ready for the trip. On May 28th, the day of departure, they will get up early. Yesterday they finished packing the suitcases. They must be at the airport at 7:30 pm.

They will get the boarding passes at the airport. Since they will have to wait, they will go to the coffee shop for breakfast. If they have more time, they will read a newspaper until it is time to depart. Later they will board the plain through gate 12. On entering the plane, a stewardess will greet them at the door and will indicate them to their seats. After placing the small suitcase on the upper storage compartment, they will take their seats and fasten their belts. The plane will take off at 10:45 sharp. The trip will last 9 hours. The plane will land in London the following day in the morning.

## C2. Read and Listen to the dialog.

*Ray **is** an American citizen, **isn't** he?*
Yes, he **is** because he was born in America.

*Julie **isn't** German, **is** she?*
No, as far as I know, she **isn't**. She's American.

*Although their friends are German, they **live** in London, **don't** they?*
Yes, they **do**. They enjoy living in London.

***They'll** get up early on the day of departure, **won't** they?*
Yes, they **will**. They have everything ready for the trip.

*The plane won't take off at 12:00 midnight, **will** it?*
No, it **won't**. It will take off at 10:45 am sharp.

**D1.** Henry (work) / Spain

*Does Henry work?*
Yes, he does.

*Yesterday he worked in England.*
Tomorrow he will work in Spain.

*Where is he going to work afterwards?*
He doesn't know yet.

**D2.** students (fly) / lake

*Do the students fly?*
Yes, they do.

*Yesterday they flew over the mountains.*
Tomorrow they will fly over the lake.

*Where are they going to fly afterwards?*
They don't know yet.

**D3.** Cindy (cook) / meat

*Does Cindy cook?*
Yes, she does.

*Yesterday she cooked fish.*
Tomorrow she will cook meat.

*What is she going to cook afterwards?*
She doesn't know yet.

**D4.** you (swim) / river

*Do you swim?*
Yes, I do.

*Yesterday I swam in the lake.*
Tomorrow I will swim in the river.

*Where are you going to swim afterwards?*
I don't know yet.

## Verb "to back"

1. Will you **back** me **up** all the time?
2. Please, don't **back out** from your word.
3. **Back off** behind that line.

## Verb "to brush"

1. I am going to **brush up** the speech.
2. **Brush that aside**.
3. **Brush off** the dandruff from your coat.

## Verb "to hang"

1. **Hang in** there.
2. He often **hangs out around** here.
3. **Hang up** the phone.

**Phrasal verbs** or **prepositional verbs** are verbs followed by a preposition or an adverb. When the verb is followed by a preposition or adverb, the verb acquires a different meaning from the original meaning. When the object of the phrasal verb is a direct object pronoun, the pronoun is placed between the verb and the preposition.

For the English audio pronunciations and written native language translations of **section E,** please go to:

## www.basicesl.com

**Back off** behind that line.

**Brush off** the dandruff from your coat.

End of the **oral exercises** for lesson 15.

**You can find additional exercises in sections D, F & G at Basic ESL Online.**

Please continue with the **written exercises** for this lesson in **section H.**

**Lesson**

# 15

## H1. Write the past tense of these irregular verbs.

| | | | | |
|---|---|---|---|---|
| 1. | tell | _____ | swim | _____ |
| 2. | think | _____ | sweep | _____ |
| 3. | throw | _____ | strike | _____ |
| 4. | wake | _____ | sting | _____ |
| 5. | win | _____ | stinks | _____ |
| 6. | wear | _____ | swear | _____ |
| 7. | write | _____ | take | _____ |

## H2. Verbs: Future Tense: Contractions

| | | | |
|---|---|---|---|
| 1. | **I will wear** a black suit. | *I'll wear* | |
| 2. | **I will not wear** jeans. | *I'll not wear* | *I won't wear* |
| 3. | **You will sit** on the floor. | _____ | _____ |
| 4. | **You will not sit** on the couch. | _____ | _____ |
| 5. | **She will ride** the train. | _____ | _____ |
| 6. | **She will not ride** the bus. | _____ | _____ |
| 7. | **We will write** letters. | _____ | _____ |
| 8. | **We will not write** postcards. | _____ | _____ |
| 9. | **They will drink** coffee. | _____ | _____ |
| 10. | **They will not drink** liquor. | _____ | _____ |

## H3. Future Tense: Change to questions.

1. **He'll** wear a black suit.        *Will he* wear a black suit?

2. **He won't** wear jeans.        _____

3. **You'll** sit on the floor.        _____

4. **You will** not sit on the couch.        _____

5. **She'll** ride the train.        _____

6. **He won't** ride the bus.        _____

7. **We'll** write letters.        _____

8. **We won't** write postcards.        _____

## H4. Future Tense: Complete with tag questions.

1. **He'll** wear a black suit,        *won't he?*

2. **He won't** wear jeans,        _____

3. **You'll** sit on the floor,        _____

4. **You will** not sit on the couch,        _____

5. **She'll** ride the train,        _____

6. **He won't** ride the bus,        _____

7. **We'll** write letters,        _____

8. **We won't** write postcards,        _____

9. Jim and I **cannot** talk to you,        _____

10. The phone **doesn't** work,        _____

11. The boys **must** leave the office,        _____

12. The boys **mustn't** come back,        _____

13. Ray **shouldn't** move to Florida,        _____

14. His family **should** stay here,        _____

15. Carla **is going** to ride the train,        _____

16. She **won't** ride the bus,        _____

## H5. Answer with short answers.

| | | Yes, I did. | No, I didn't |
|---|---|---|---|
| 1. | Did you hide the money? | | |
| 2. | Will she be there? | _____ | _____ |
| 3. | Does John teach math? | _____ | _____ |
| 4. | Are you hungry now? | _____ | _____ |
| 5. | Won't you forgive Ann? | _____ | _____ |
| 6. | Is Tom still stealing? | _____ | _____ |
| 7. | Should I tell him that? | _____ | _____ |
| 8. | Do the students understand it? | _____ | _____ |

## H6. Use the auxiliary verbs do, does and did for emphasis.

1. I **taught** German.  *I did teach German.*
2. We **flew** around the world.  _____
3. They **climbed** the mountain.  _____
4. We **swam** in the ocean.  _____
5. Andy **crosses** the jungle on foot.  _____
6. A man **got l**ost there.  _____
7. Many **drown** in the lake.  _____
8. He **fought** against a crocodile.  _____

## H7. Make the object of the verb the subject of the sentence.

1. **I** didn't ask **you** a question.  *You asked me a question.*
2. He didn't give **us** presents.  _____
3. She didn't see **them**.  _____
4. We didn't know **him**.  _____
5. You didn't forget **her**.  _____
6. They didn't find **me**.  _____
7. She won't call **us**.  _____

## H8. Follow the example.

1. Henry / travel / India

**England**

*Does Henry **travel**?*
*Yes, he **travels.***

*Yesterday he **traveled** to India.*
*Tomorrow he **will travel** to England.*

2. Jenifer / sing / church

**school**

_____
_____
_____
_____

3. friends / cook / meat

**fish**

_____
_____
_____
_____

4. you-Sara / swim / river

**ocean**

_____
_____
_____
_____

5. Monica / teach / math

**music**

_____
_____
_____
_____

# ANSWER KEY SECTION

# BASIC ESL WORKBOOK LEVEL 3

## H1

1. stronger     the strongest
2. easier     the easiest
3. nicer     the nicest
4. bigger     the biggest
5. worse     the worst
6. more beautiful     the most beautiful
7. more unhappy     the most unhappy
8. larger     the largest
9. smaller     the smallest
10. prettier     the prettiest
11. better     the best
12. heavier     the heaviest
13. farther     the farthest
14. more dangerous     the most dangerous
15. more     the most
16. less     the least
17. more colorful     the most colorful
18. more fertile     the most fertile

## H2

1. The pine tree is the tallest tree of all.
2. The oak wood is the most expensive wood in the store.
3. The bamboo is the ugliest three of all.
4. The cactus is the most dangerous plant in the garden.
5. The roses are the most beautiful flowers in the market.
6. Cindy is the smartest girl of the three sisters.

## H3

1. in
2. in
3. of
4. in
5. in
6. of
7. of
8. in
9. in
10. of
11. in

## H4

1. as
2. younger
3. more
4. the most
5. the most
6. more
7. as
8. most
9. than

## H5

1. worse
   the worst
2. farther
   the farthest
3. better
   the best
4. more
   the most
5. less
   the least

## H6

**1.**
The dog is big.
The lion is bigger than the dog.
The giraffe is the biggest animal in the zoo.

**2.**
The olive tree is tall.
The oak tree is taller than the olive tree.
The pine tree is the tallest tree in the forest.

**3.**
The boar is aggressive.
The bear is more aggressive than the boar.
The tiger is the most aggressive animal of the three.

**4.**
The lily is pretty.
The daisy is prettier than the lily.
The tulip is the prettiest flower of all.

**5.**
The cheese is good.
The pie is better than the cheese.
The apple is the best dessert in the restaurant.

# H1

| | |
|---|---|
| 1. cost | built |
| 2. covered | bet |
| 3. dug | handled |
| 4. filled | put |
| 5. caught | cut |
| 6. maintained | weighed |
| 7. picked | discussed |
| 8. placed | blew |
| 9. planted | committed |
| 10. chose | broke |
| 11. prevented | revealed |
| 12. provided | expected |
| 13. bought | bent |
| 14. pulled | watered |
| 15. trimmed | brought |
| 16. did | strengthened |

# H2

1. He did not plant a tree.
2. We did not break two picks.
3. Mary did not do homework.
4. She did not play at school.
5. We did not build that house.
6. The house did not cost a lot.
7. They did not dig three holes.
8. The pot did not weigh....
9. She did not break the rake.
10. Fred did not catch a fish.
11. Mom did not trim the ....
12. Dad did not cut a small tree.

# H3

1. Did Sara water ....
2. Did he choose...
3. Did they do ....
4. Did dad mow ...
5. Did his son bet...
6. Did mom pull...
7. Did a strong wind blow...
8. Did we buy ...
9. Did Greg bend...
10. Did Ray use ...
11. Did Edward bring...

# H4

1. Yes, she watered the plants.
   No, she did not water the plants.
2. Yes, he mowed the lawn.
   No, he did not mow the lawn.
3. Yes, he dug some holes.
   No, he did not dig any holes.
4. Yes, I brought some tools.
   No, I did not bring any tools.
5. Yes, she bet some money.
   No, she did not bet any money.
6. Yes, he broke the pick.
   No, he did not break the pick.
7. Yes, he bought another one.
   No, he did not buy another one.
8. Yes, he pulled the weeds.
   No, he did not pull the weeds.
9. Yes, the two boys helped.
   No, the two boys did not help.
10. Yes, they did some work.
    No, they did not do any work.
11. Yes, they weighed the bags.
    No, they did not weigh the bags.
12. Yes, they cut some roses.
    No, they did not cut any roses.
13. Yes, they picked up the trash.
    No, they did not pick up the trash.

# H5

Last Saturday Charles, my oldest son, was in charge of maintaining the garden neat and clean. He started to work in the garden early. First of all, he trimmed the bushes and the trees. Then he planted trees and plants. He purchased the plants from the nursery.

Afterwards he pulled out the weeds. He used a light hoe and a heavy pick. When he finished pulling out the weeds, he picked up the leaves from the ground. He put the trash in plastic bags. The black garden bags are the biggest of all.

Last Saturday, Chuck filled three plastic bags with trash. Each one weighed 45 pounds.

## H1

| | |
|---|---|
| 1. bore | clang |
| 2. beat | caught |
| 3. became | dug |
| 4. began | fed |
| 5. cost | burst |
| 6. bled | broke |
| 7. bit | brought |
| 8. grew | bought |

## H2

1. What did he bring?
2. Whom did the dog bite?
3. How many tractors did they buy?
4. What are the tractors like?
5. With what did he plow the land?
6. When did Lydia begin to work?
7. Who grew lots of onions?
8. How did the onions taste?

## H3

1. You don't walk early ...
2. Fred cannot plow the land.
3. Carol did not walk home...
4. I may not see you tomorrow.
5. Tony did not dig three holes.
6. He does not like to work...
7. My brother did not feed
8. I am not feeding the ...
9. They might not sell the ...
10. She could not remember ...
11. Jennifer did not sow ...
12. He is not tilling the land ...

## H4

1. Did you walk early to the field?
2. Can Fred plow the land?
3. Did Carol walk home late?
4. May I see you tomorrow?
5. Did Tony dig three holes?
6. Does he like to work in the ...?
7. Did my brother feed the ...?
8. Am I feeding the animals...?
9. Might they sell the barn?
10. Could she remember you?
11. May she go home now?

## H5

| | |
|---|---|
| 1. Yes, I did. | No, I didn't. |
| 2. Yes, they are. | No, they aren't. |
| 3. Yes, they can. | No, they can't. |
| 4. Yes, he may. | No, he may not. |
| 5. Yes, she does. | No, she doesn't. |
| 6. Yes, she could. | No, she couldn't. |
| 7. Yes, she is | No, she isn't. |
| 8. Yes, she might. | No, she might not. |
| 9. Yes, she did. | No, she didn't. |
| 10. Yes, I am. | No, I'm not. |

## H6

1. My pen is more expensive than yours.
2. John weighs more than Ann.
3. We are as old as Lisa.
4. My desk is wider than yours.
5. This book is thinner than that one.
6. My pool is deeper than the river.

## H7

1. rose
2. rose
3. oak tree
4. cactus
5. pick
6. tulip
7. trunk

## H8

| | |
|---|---|
| 1. pulled | 8. the tallest |
| 2. waters | 9. as |
| 3. may | 10. younger |
| 4. uses | 11. than |
| 5. bring | 12. than |
| 6. is picking | 13. of |
| 7. taller | 14. grew |

# H1

1. drove    built
2. drank    ground
3. drew    cut
4. ate    blew
5. fell    broke
6. heard    bent
7. fed    brought
8. felt    bled

# H2

1. the boy's eyes
2. the boys' eyes
3. Mary's eyes
4. Fred's hand
5. the man's hands
6. the men's hands
7. the girls' hands
8. Carol's head

# H3

1. The child's hand is infected.
2. Paul's leg is getting better.
3. My uncle's teeth are yellow.
4. Liz's ears are plugged.
5. The man's neck is stiff.
6. I like Jane' hair.
7. The women's hats are blue.
8. Ann's tongue is white.
9. Joe's clothes are expensive.
10. The boys' feet are dirty.

# H4

1. They are Margaret's lips.
2. I am driving my father's car.
3. I drew Jenifer's face.
4. He drank his sister's medicine.
5. It ate the baby's food.
6. They swallowed their aunt's pills.
7. It built the teacher's house.

# H5

**1.**
Whose lips are these?
They are my sister's lips.
She kisses with her lips.

**3.**
Whose eye is this?
This is the woman's eye.
She sees with her eyes.

**5.**
Whose foot is this?
It is Tom's foot.
He walks with his feet.

**2.**
Whose noses are these?
They are the girls' noses.
They smell with their noses.

**4.**
Whose ears are these?
They are the women's ears.
They hear with their ears.

# H6

1. We find the hair and the face.
2. Yes, they are.
3. They are below the nose.
4. It is located inside the mouth.
5. No, it does not belong to the neck.
6. The function of the neck is to support the head.
7. The throat is part of the neck.
8. We use our hands to pick up objects.
9. No, the leg does not include the elbow.

# H1

| | |
|---|---|
| 1. found | drove |
| 2. forbade | drank |
| 3. forgot | drew |
| 4. flew | ate |
| 5. forecast | fell |
| 6. fled | heard |
| 7. froze | fed |
| 8. forgave | felt |

# H2

1. You ought to clean...
2. They ought to cut...
3. She ought to stretch...
4. He ought to stop...
5. Tom ought to check...
6. I ought to polish...
7. We ought to strengthen...
8. You ought to clear...

# H3

1. Cindy did not forget...
2. You should not see...
3. Mary did not forgive...
4. I ought not to eat more.
5. I cannot walk far.
6. Henry did not call Liz...
7. She did not feel any pain.
8. The boys were not at home.
9. The doctor did not fly...
10. He may not return soon.
11. He doesn't go there often.
12. I did not freeze the juice.

# H4

1. Did Cindy forget...?
2. Should I see your cousin?
3. Did Mary forgive...?
4. Does Fred have to eat more?
5. Can I walk far?
6. Did Henry call ...?
7. Did she feel any pain?
8. Were the boys at home?
9. Did the doctor fly to ...?
10. May he return soon?
11. Does he go there often?
12. Did I freeze the juice?

# H5

| | | |
|---|---|---|
| 1. | Yes, I am. | No, I'm not. |
| 2. | Yes, you should. | No, you shouldn't. |
| 3. | Yes, you can. | No, you can't. |
| 4. | Yes, she did. | No, she didn't. |
| 5. | Yes, you may. | No, you may not. |
| 6. | Yes, It is. | No, it isn't. |
| 7. | Yes, she should. | No, she shouldn't |
| 8. | Yes, she does. | No, she doesn't. |
| 9. | Yes, she could. | No, she couldn't. |
| 10. | Yes, I do. | No, I don't. |
| 11. | Yes, I am. | No, I'm not. |

# H6

1. I like Paul's sweater.
2. You like the wall color.
3. What's the page number?
4. This is my uncle's picture.
5. Look at the ceiling lamp.
6. I drive the girls' white car.
7. We enjoy Mrs. Gray's class.
8. We love the art class.
9. The boys' noses are big.
10. I like the bedroom furniture.
11. We don't use plastic cups.
12. I hate Tom's paper plates.
13. Are the city parks closed?

# H7

1. Is Frank's sister sick?
   Yes, she is sick.
   What is wrong with his sister?
   Her stomach hurts.
   Shouldn't she see the doctor now?
   In my opinion she should.
3. Is Paul's aunt sick?
   Yes, she is sick.
   What is wrong with her?
   Her throat hurts.
   Shouldn't she see the doctor now?
   In my opinion she should.

2. Are the boys' parents sick?
   Yes, they are sick.
   What is wrong with their parents?
   Their backs hurt.
   Shouldn't they see the doctor now?
   In my opinion they should.
4. Are Cynthia's nephews sick?
   Yes, they are.
   What is wrong with her nephews?
   Their bones hurt.
   Shouldn't they see the doctor now?
   In my opinion they should.

# H1

1. hid     drove
2. held     drank
3. ground     drew
4. fought     ate
5. beat     fell
6. bit     heard
7. grew     fed
8. became     felt

# H2

1. You have to take
2. She doesn't have to rest
3. Mom has to cover
4. Tony doesn't have to stop
5. I have to go
6. Mom has to talk
7. We have to wait
8. We don't have to be

# H3

1. Mary did not fight fiercely.
2. You should not ignore the advice.
3. They ought not to eat more.
4. I cannot walk far.
5. Henry did not hide under the bed.
6. She did not drink some water.
7. I must not have an operation.
8. I don't have to take these pills.

# H4

1. Did Mary fight fiercely?
2. Should you ignore the advice?
3. Ought they eat more?
4. Can I walk far?
5. Did Henry hide under the bed?
6. Does she drink some water?
7. Must I have an operation?
8. Do I have to take these pills?

# H5

1. She must be tired.
2. He must be sad.
3. They must be hungry.
4. He must be slow.
5. She must be smart.
6. She must be sick.
7. They must be proud.

# H6

| | | | |
|---|---|---|---|
| 1. | B | A | C |
| 2. | A | C | B |
| 3. | B | A | C |
| 4. | B | A | B |
| 5. | B | A | A |
| 6. | B | A | C |
| 7. | A | B | C |

# H7

1. may, can
2. should, ought to
3. can, may
4. should, ought to
5. may, can
6. must, has to
7. may
8. should, can
9. should
10. must

# H8

1. Alice is Mrs. Brown's small daughter.
2. Alice is hurt in bed.
3. She twisted her ankle.
4. The doctor examined Alice's ankle.
5. The doctor advised Alice to rest at home.
6. She rested at home for six days.

# H9

1. children's
2. man's
3. Nancy's
4. family
5. Lynn's
6. shouldn't
7. have
8. ought
9. Can
10. must

# H1

1. kept      got
2. left      fell
3. lost      heard
4. made      felt
5. knelt      hid
6. led      held
7. lent      ground
8. lit, lighted      fought

# H2

1. There are twenty-four hours in a day.
2. There are sixty minutes in one hour.
3. There are 15 minutes in a quarter of an hour.
4. There are sixty seconds in one minute.

# H3

1. It is two o'clock in the morning.
2. It is twelve o'clock noon.
3. It is one thirty in the afternoon.
4. It is six fifteen in the evening.
5. It is nine forty-five at night.
6. It is twelve o'clock midnight

# H4

1. in      far
2. off      at
3. with      in
4. up      in
5. to      by
6. on      at
7. about      for
8. to      for
9. to      from
10. at      with
11. until      in
12. on      for

# H5

**1.**
**What is it now?**
It is six fifteen in the morning.
**At what time does Ann get up?**
She gets up at seven o'clock in the morning.

**2.**
**What time is it now?**
It is nine thirty in the morning.
**At what time does Ann eat breakfast?**
She eats breakfast at eight fifteen in the morning.

**3.**
**What time is it now?**
It is twelve o'clock noon.
At what time does Ann have lunch?
She has lunch at twelve thirty in the afternoon.

**4.**
**What time is it now?**
It is five ten in the evening.
**At what time does Ann study?**
She studies at five forty-five in the evening.

**5.**
**What time is it now?**
It is eight twenty at night.
**At what time does Ann go to bed?**
She goes to bed at nine o'clock at night.

# H6

**Yesterday** my two brothers Mike and Tom **were** still sleeping at 7:00 am, when they heard the alarm clock. Once in a while they arrive at school late because the clock is ten minutes slow. Their first class **began** at 8:30.

The school bell **rang** at 9:15 for a ten minute break. At 9:25 they **came** back to the math class. They **did** lots of math problems. They **solved** all the problems in half an hour.

The students **went** to the cafeteria for lunch at noon time. After lunch they **had** three quarters of an hour to play on the playground.

The last class **ended** at 2:45 pm. They **left** school for home at 3:15 pm.

## H1

| | |
|---|---|
| 1. paid | kept |
| 2. met | left |
| 3. quit | lost |
| 4. put | made |
| 5. read | knelt |
| 6. rang, rung | led |
| 7. rose | lent |
| 8. meant | lit, lighted |

## H2

1. I know her.
2. I know him.
3. I know it.
4. I know him.
5. I know her.
6. I know them.
7. I know them.
8. I know them.

## H3

1. My brother wears it.
2. Tony lives with her.
3. Her uncle knows us.
4. Don't open it yet.
5. I saw him last week.
6. I also met her.
7. She was with them.
8. She answered them.
9. She is living with her.
10. I paid them.
11. We met her.
12. Please, don't ring it.

## H4

1. He fears them.
2. She loves it.
3. He lost it.
4. They quit them.
5. It canceled them.
6. He punished them.
7. He was upset with him.
8. They are working for him.
9. He bought them.
10. He likes them.
11. They don't bother us.

## H5

1. them.
2. me.
3. it.
4. her.
5. them.
6. him?
7. it?

## H6

1. He likes it very much.
2. She wants them now.
3. They belong to Bob's uncle.
4. He eats with us.
5. You do not need him.
6. I met Tony's sister in church.
7. What day of the week is today?

## H7

1. Look it up in the book.
2. The lion tore them off.
3. The city tears them down.
4. He threw it up.
5. Don't give them up.
6. Please, put them out.
7. Why don't you help her out?

## H8

**1.**
Did Steve put off the trip?
Yes, he put it off.
When did he put off the trip?
He put it off Sunday.

**2.**
Did you cross out the mistakes?
Yes, I crossed them out.
When did you cross out the mistakes?
I crossed them out on Monday.

**3.**
Did mom wake up her daughter?
Yes, she woke her up.
When did she wake up her daughter?
She woke her up on Tuesday.

**4.**
Did Ann tear up the letters?
Yes, she tore them up.
When did she tear up the letters?
She tore them up last weekend.

**5.**
Did Greg give away his car?
Yes, he gave it away.
When did he give away his car?
He gave it away yesterday.

# H1

| | |
|---|---|
| 1. rid | paid |
| 2. ran | met |
| 3. saw | quit |
| 4. sought | put |
| 5. set | read |
| 6. sat | rang |
| 7. spun | rose |
| 8. spread | meant |

# H2

1. on June twenty second.
   on the twenty second of June.
2. the first of October.
   on October first.
3. on the third of December.
   on December third.
4. in May.
5. on Monday.

# H3

1. on May fifth two thousand and five.
2. on January thirteen nineteen hundred and eighty.
3. on March third thirteen hundred and twenty.
4. on February fourteen eighteen hundred and thirty.
5. on December twelfth seventeen hundred and seventy nine.
6. on June sixth two thousand and eleven.

# H4

1. When is your birthday?
2. What day is today?
3. Whose birthday was yesterday?
4. What did his dad give him?
5. What were the gifts like?
6. How many gifts did Tony get?
7. What time did the party begin?
8. How long did it last?
9. Who felt very happy?
10. How did Tony also feel?
11. When did he arrive home?

# H5

1. Yes, he read them.
2. Yes, I sat on it.
3. Yes, he set them.
4. Yes, she paid them.
5. Yes, I saw her.
6. Yes, I got rid of him.
7. Yes, she sought it.
8. Yes, I woke them up.
9. Yes, she kept it.
10. Yes, she lost it.
11. Yes, I spread them.

# H6

1. He was the first President of the United States.
2. He was President from 1789 to 1797.
3. He was a soldier.
4. It ended in 1783.
5. He married Martha Curtis.
6. He was 67 years old.

# H7

1. In the morning
2. Thursday
3. Noon
4. 52
5. February
6. Sunday

# H8

| | | | |
|---|---|---|---|
| 1. She | | 7. at | |
| 2. Her | | 8. wants | |
| 3. her | | 9. want | |
| 4. her | | 10. come | |
| 5. at | | 11. them | |
| 6. in | | 12. They | |

# H1

1. laid      rid
2. rode      ran
3. said      saw
4. sold      sought
5. sent      set
6. shot      sat
7. shed      spun
8. shone     spread

# H2

1. It is very cold today.      It was very cold yesterday.
2. It is raining today.        It rained yesterday.
3. It is sunny today.          It was sunny yesterday.
4. It is hot today.            It was hot yesterday.
5. It is snowing today.        It snowed yesterday.
6. It is foggy today.          It was foggy yesterday.
7. It is drizzling today.      It was drizzling yesterday.
8. It is freezing today.       It was freezing yesterday.
9. It is hailing today.        It hailed yesterday.

# H3

1. I **always** get up early.
2. I am **always** there at noon.
3. He came to school **late**.
4. He is **seldom** wrong.
5. There is no class **today**.
6. He **seldom** studies at home.
7. Did you **ever** say bad words?
8. We **usually** don't say them.
9. He is **usually** in his room.
10. I am not working **now**.
11. Greg **often** sits on that chair.
12. He is **often** tired.
13. John did not come **early**.
14. They are **rarely** there on...
15. He **rarely** eats on Sundays.
16. We **still** work here.
17. We are **still** at lunch.
18. He saw his uncles **once**.
19. He **hardly** knows them.
20. They were here **yesterday**.
21. She plans to come **soon**.
22. She promised it **twice**.
23. Henry **generally** cooks on ...
24. Mom is **generally** busy.
25. I am **still** sick in bed.
26. I'm not well **yet**.

# H4

1. He kept them apart.
2. Germany took it over.
3. The teachers brake them up.
4. Don't tear it up.
5. Please, turn them on.
6. Throw them away.
7. Don't give it away.
8. Don't hang it up.

# H5

1. I did see and elephant in...
2. They did run ten miles
3. We did sit on the snow...
4. You do sell cars for John.
5. It did stop suddenly.
6. She does ride the train...
7. Tony did mean that.
8. We did lend you $1,000.

# H6

1. How is the weather in August?
2. He sold it yesterday
3. She seldom wears sandals.
4. The weather can be hot.
5. It is still cold in February.
6. What is the weather like now?
7. They shot him yesterday.

# H7

1. my       yours
2. his      mine
3. her      our
4. our      hers
5. her      ours
6. my       theirs
7. their    their
8. their    my
9. our      ours

# H8

1. There is a variety of climate conditions.
2. It is a beautiful state.
3. It ends in March.
4. The average temperature is 85 degrees.
5. It depends on how close is the ocean.
6. It can be hot.

# H1

1. shrank    shook
2. shut    lent
3. sang    said
4. slept    sold
5. slid    sent
6. spoke    shot
7. sped    shed
8. spent    shone

# H2

1. nobody    nobody
2. no one    no one
3. nothing    far
4. nowhere    less
5. nobody    little
6. nobody    few
7. neither of them    close
8. none of them    worse
9. nothing    least

# H3

1. Yes, he lent it.
2. Yes, he sold them.
3. Yes, she spoke to them.
4. Yes, they sat on it.
5. Yes, they rode it.
6. Yes, they stole it.
7. Yes, I swept them.
8. Yes, it shook it.
9. Yes, it hit them.
10. Yes, they slept on it.
11. Yes, she sang it.
12. Yes, he spent it.
13. Yes, they sent it.
14. Yes, she shed them.

# H4

1. He drank no milk.
2. We said no words.
3. Jane sold no houses.
4. Carol sang no songs.
5. Mom opened no doors.
6. Henry heard nothing.
7. Fred knew no answers.
8. We ate no mushrooms.

# H5

1. No, I didn't see anybody.
   No, I saw nobody.
2. No, they didn't shoot anyone.
   No, they shot no one.
3. No, I didn't get anything.
   No, I got nothing.
4. No, he didn't say any words.
   No, he said no words.
5. No, he wasn't anywhere.
   No, he was nowhere.
6. No, they didn't kill anybody.
   No, they killed nobody.

# H6

1. F
2. E
3. H
4. J
5. D
6. G
7. I
8. B
9. C
10. K
11. A

# H7

1. Tony is younger than Alice.
2. They got married on June 1st, 1968.
3. They took a cruise to celebrate their 25th wedding anniversary.
4. They boarded the ship in the evening.
5. It was nice.
6. They were relaxing on the deck of the boat.

# H8

1. goes
2. seldom
3. every day
4. still
5. yet
6. often
7. it
8. us
9. sleep
10. Who

# H1

1. stole   shrank
2. spat    shut
3. stuck   sang
4. sprang  sank
5. stood   slept
6. strove  slid
7. tore    spoke
8. wept    sped

# H2

1. ... I will eat
2. ... he will spit
3. ... he will study
4. ... she will ride
5. ... it will be
6. ... she will sleep
7. ... we will see
8. ... they will kneel
9. ... I will speak

# H3

**A**
1. go
2. am going
3. went
4. will go

**B**
1. works
2. is working
3. worked
4. will work

**C**
1. sweep
2. are sweeping
3. swept
4. will sweep

**D**
1. sleeps
2. is sleeping
3. slept
4. will sleep

**E**
1. forgets
2. is forgetting
3. forgot
4. will forget

**F**
1. steal
2. are stealing
3. stole
4. will steal

# H4

1. Clair is not working now.
2. She will not work until five.
3. Yesterday she did not work late.
4. She does not usually work late.
5. Today she cannot leave earlier.
6. She must not arrive home soon.
7. She will not ride the bus home.
8. She may not walk home.

# H5

1. Is Clair working now?
2. Will she work until five?
3. Did she work late yesterday?
4. Does she usually work late?
5. Can she leave earlier today?
6. Must she arrive home soon?
7. Will she ride the bus home?
8. May she walk home now?

# H6

1. I am going to stop...
2. We are going to swim...
3. We are not going to ...
4. Greg is not going to....
5. The boys are going to fly...
6. The girls are going to stay..
7. It is going to be cold...

# H7

**Last year** Laura's father **went** to Europe. He **visited** several countries. He **began** his trip in Germany. From there he **flew** to France.

After spending one week in Paris, he **took** the train to England. He **crossed** the English Channel by boat. Ten days later he **came** back to Paris after visiting London, York and Glasgow. He **rented** a car in Paris and **drove** south to Spain.

It **took** him three days to arrive in Madrid, the capital of Spain. It **was** very cold in Madrid during the month of February. This is why he **bought** a warm overcoat in one of the best stores of the city. He **paid** for it with the American Express card.

## H1

1. took      stole
2. swam      spat
3. swept     stuck
4. struck    sprang
5. stung     stood
6. stank     strove
7. swore     tore
8. taught    wept

## H2

1. What did you that for?
2. Whom do you work for?
3. Whom did you go with?
4. Whom are they fighting against?
5. What are you talking about?
6. What is she thinking of?
7. Where is your aunt going to?
8. What did she step on?

## H3

1. does he not?
2. does he?
3. doesn't she?
4. doesn't he?
5. does he?
6. don't I?
7. do I?

## H4

1. did he not?
2. did he?
3. did she not?
4. didn't he?
5. did he?
6. didn't I
7. did I

## H5

1. Will he not?
2. Will he?
3. Will she not?
4. Will he not?
5. Will he?
6. Will I not?
7. Will I?

## H6

1. You don't come from France, do you?
   - Yes, I do.
   But you don't live in France, do you?
   - No, I don't.

2. Cecilia and Patty come from Mexico, don't they?
   - Yes, they do.
   But they don't live in Mexico, do they?
   - No, they don't.

3. Keiko and you don't come from Japan, do you?
   - Yes, we do.
   But you don't live in Japan, do you?
   - No, I don't.

4. Kate doesn't come from Spain, does she?
   - Yes, she does.
   But she doesn't live in Spain, does she?
   - No, she doesn't.

5. Carlos doesn't come from Sweden, does he?
   - Yes, he does.
   But he doesn't live in Sweden, does he?
   - No, he doesn't.

## H7

Next year Richard **will go** to Europe. First, he **will make** a visit to a friend in Sweden. From Sweden he **will fly** to Greece.

He **will spend** one week in Athens, its capital. Then he **will take** the train to Switzerland. There he **will get** on a bus to Hungary. Two days later he **will take** a river cruise through several European countries.

Richard **will arrive** in Holland five days later. In Holland, he **will rent** a car and **will drive** to Belgium. It **will be** very cold in Brussels during the month of February when he arrives. This is why he **will buy** an overcoat in the city.

He **will feel** tired at the end of the trip. He **will sleep** in the plane on his way back to United States.

## H1

| | |
|---|---|
| 1. told | swam |
| 2. thought | swept |
| 3. threw | struck |
| 4. woke | stung |
| 5. won | stank |
| 6. wore | swore |
| 7. wrote | took |
| 8. wove | taught |

## H2

1. studying
2. going
3. listening
4. warning
5. answering
6. closing
7. speaking
8. stealing
9. traveling

## H3

1. is he not?
2. is he?
3. are they not?
4. are they?
5. am I not?
6. am I?
7. weren't you?
8. were you?
9. wasn't she?
10. was she?
11. will we not?
12. will be?

## H4

1. can't you?
2. can you?
3. couldn't they?
4. could they?
5. shouldn't i?
6. should i?
7. wouldn't she?
8. would she?
9. mustn't we?
10. must we?
11. ought he not?
12. ought he?

## H5

1. at, with
2. on, on
3. on top, on
4. at, on, by
5. up, on
6. to, about
7. up, at, in
8. at, in
9. to, at

## H6

1. their
2. them, my
3. I, my
4. theirs
5. they, theirs
6. them, they

## H7

1. Yes, they did. They brought it.
2. Yes, he did. He chose it.
3. Yes, she did. She forgave him.
4. Yes, she did. She spoke to her.
5. Yes, they did. They paid them.
6. Yes, they did. They told her that.
7. Yes, he did. He wrote them.
8. Yes, I did. I threw them away.

## H8

**1.**
I am not American, am I?
No, you aren't.
I am German, am I not?
Yes, you are.

**2.**
The students are not Italian, are they?
No, they aren't.
They are Chinese, are they not?
Yes, they are.

**3.**
Henry is not Polish, is he?
No, he isn't.
He is Russian, isn't he?
Yes, he is.

**4.**
They women are Dutch, aren't they?
No, they aren't.
They are Japanese, aren't they?
Yes, they are.

**5.**
The daughter is not French, is she?
No, she isn't.
She is Mexican, isn't she?
Yes, she is.

# H1

1. told     swam
2. thought   swept
3. threw    struck
4. woke     stung
5. won      stank
6. wore     swore
7. wrote    took

# H2

1. I'll wear
2. I'll not wear     I won't wear
3. You'll sit
4. You'll not sit     You won't sit
5. She'll ride
6. She'll not ride     She won't ride
7. We'll write
8. We'll not write     We won't write
9. They'll drink
10. They'll not drink     The won't drink

# H3

1. Will he wear a black suit?
2. Won't he wear jeans?
3. Will you sit on the floor?
4. Will you not sit on the couch?
5. Will she ride the train?
6. Won't she ride the bus?
7. Will they write letters?
8. Won't we write postcards?

# H4

1. won't he?
2. will he?
3. won't you?
4. will you?
5. won't she?
6. will he?
7. won't we?
8. will we?
9. can we?
10. does it?
11. mustn't they?
12. must they?
13. should he?
14. shouldn't it?
15. isn't she?
16. will she?

# H5

1. Yes, I did.     No, I didn't.
2. Yes, she will     No, she won't.
3. Yes, he does.     No, he doesn't.
4. Yes, I am.     No, I'm not.
5. Yes, I will.     No, I won't.
6. Yes, he is.     No, he isn't.
7. Yes, you should.     No, you shouldn't.
8. Yes, they do.     No, they don't.

# H6

1. I did teach German.
2. We did fly around the world.
3. They did climb the highest...
4. We did swim in the middle...
5. Andy does cross the jungle...
6. A man did get lost there.
7. Many do drown in the lake.
8. He did fight against a ...

# H7

1. You asked me a question.
2. We gave him presents.
3. They saw her.
4. He knew us.
5. She forgot you.
6. I found them.
7. We will call her.

# H8

**1.**
Does Henry travel?
Yes, he travels.
Yesterday, he traveled to India.
Tomorrow he will travel England.

**2.**
Does Jenifer sing?
Yes, she sings.
Yesterday, she sang in the church.
Tomorrow she will sing in the...

**3.**
Do your friends cook?
Yes, they cook.
Yesterday, they cooked meat.
Tomorrow they will cook fish.

**4.**
Do you and Sara swim?
Yes, we swim
Yesterday, we swam in the river.
Tomorrow, we will swim in the ocean.

**5.**
Does Monica teach?
Yes, she teaches.
Yesterday, she taught music.
Tomorrow she will teach math.